Yale New Classics

The Theban Plays of
Sophocles

Translated by David R. Slavitt

Yale University Press

New Haven and London

Published with assistance from the Kingsley Trust Association Publication Fund established by the Scroll and Key Society of Yale College.

Set in Adobe Garamond type by The Composing Room of Michigan, Inc. Printed in the United States of America.

Library of Congress Cataloging-in-Publication Data

Sophocles.
    [Selections. English. 2007]
    The Theban plays of Sophocles / translated by David R. Slavitt.
        p. cm.
    Includes bibliographical references.
    ISBN: 978-0-300-11776-9 (alk. paper)
    1. Sophocles—Translations into English.   2. Oedipus (Greek mythology)—Drama.   3. Antigone (Greek mythology)—Drama.   I. Slavitt, David R., 1935–   II. Title.
    PA4414.A2S53 2007
    882'.01—dc22

                                                        2006026965

A catalogue record for this book is available from the British Library.

The paper in this book meets the guidelines for permanence and durability of the Committee on Production Guidelines for Book Longevity of the Council on Library Resources.

10 9 8 7 6 5 4 3 2 1

for Don Gastwirth

Contents

Translator's Preface

This isn't a trilogy. The Theban plays were not conceived or presented as parts of a unified whole as were the plays of the *Oresteia* of Aeschylus. Instead, the story of the house of Laius was one to which Sophocles returned again and again for the bright light it could shed on the human condition. His voice changes over the years: *Oedipus at Colonus* is an old man's play, dreadful in its venomous confrontations and, at the same time, exalting in the reconciliation of its mysterious ending. It is altogether different in timbre and texture from the earlier works, and we can see in the course of the dramatist's development the outlines at least of an intellectual, artistic, and spiritual biography.

I was delighted—if also intimidated—to be invited by Yale University Press to try my hand at these masterpieces. My mentor at Andover was Dudley Fitts, and the versions that he and Robert Fitzgerald did of these masterworks seemed to me quite satisfactory and, indeed, unbeatable. But taking another look at them, I realized that they go back a long way: their *Antigone* was published in 1939. The poetic conventions and the style of that time are not those of today. Fitts's dialogue holds up pretty well, but Fitzgerald's choral odes are just a bit fussy for twenty-first-century tastes. I supposed I could not do any more harm to them than I could to Sophocles himself. So why not treat myself to an enormously rich and engaging experience? To hear these plays resound in my own sinuses and to taste them in my mouth—which is what ought to happen in a good translation—would be an almost unimaginable pleasure.

I have kept as close to the Greek as I could. There are small intrusions here and there that are, I hope, grace notes that reveal something interesting about the text. In *Oedipus at Colonus,* for instance, I stick in the words "a poet's dream" in one of the choral odes (p. 176) as a way of letting the reader know that the surrounding descriptions were recognizable to the Athenian audiences as conventional literary expressions, almost as if they were in quotes. If I could make such clarifications now and then with only a few modest words, it would be better to do so, I thought, than to litter the pages with references to endnotes. I did not want to turn these plays into one of those overcurated shows we see in some museums, where the paintings have been reduced to illustrations for the audio-guide lecture.

I am mindful of the fact that some of the readers of this book may be students to whom it has been assigned. I apologize to them and hope they can somehow overlook that unfortunate compulsion and find ways to respond to Sophocles' poetry innocently—as if they had come to these pages voluntarily and even eagerly. I have supplied a glossary of names as a convenience to readers. But the ecology of intellectual life is different now. There is hardly a proper name here that Google cannot explain in a matter of seconds. For students or general readers wishing more detailed information, the Perseus Digital Library (www.perseus.tufts.edu) offers links to almost every word, either in Greek, Greek transliterated to Roman characters (for those who cannot read the Greek alphabet or whose computers do not have Greek fonts downloaded), or in a literal translation by Sir Richard Jebb. For those who do not do computers, there is the Loeb Classical Library version, which also offers Sir Hugh Lloyd-Jones's literal translation with the Greek *en face.* There is also the *Oxford Classical Dictio-*

nary. And I am still fond of my old *Lemprière's Classical Dictionary of Proper Names Mentioned in Ancient Authors.*

I have translated the words of the play, but my hope is that in the following pages I have also translated something of my joy and awe in reading them.

Acknowledgments

I want to acknowledge the kindness and scrupulous attention that has been given to various drafts of these plays by Daniel Mark Epstein and Professor Gail Holst-Warhoft. And to Professor Dan Berman at Penn State University, who has gone over each line with a jeweler's loupe and has made innumerable suggestions for improvements large and small, I owe a particular debt. To all three I give thanks for their help and their friendship. Mistakes and lapses are, of course, my own. I also want to thank the editors of *Per Contra,* in which odes I and IV of *Oedipus Tyrranos* first appeared.

Antigone

Dramatis Personae

ANTIGONE	daughter and half-sister of Oedipus
ISMENE	sister of Antigone
CHORUS	of elders of Thebes
CREON	Antigone's uncle (brother of Jocasta, Antigone's mother)
GUARD	one of those sent to watch over Polyneices' corpse
TIRESIAS	the blind prophet of Apollo
HAEMON	son of Creon and Eurydice, fiancé of Antigone
MESSENGER	a servant of Creon's
SECOND MESSENGER	another in Creon's household
EURYDICE	Creon's wife, Haemon's mother

Silent Roles

ATTENDANTS	of Creon
GUARDS	of Antigone, after her arrest
SERVANTS	of Eurydice
BOY	Tiresias's guide

Prologue

[The gateway of the palace of Thebes. ANTIGONE enters from the
left, which is the direction of the city. She whistles what is a
prearranged signal. ISMENE enters from the center, which is to say,
from the interior of the palace.]

ANTIGONE
Dear sister, Ismene, what evils that come
from Oedipus our father has Zeus not sent
to burden our lives? There is nothing, no shame, no pain,
no sorrow, no disgrace that you and I
have not endured. And now comes the general's new
proclamation. What have you heard? Or do you
take no notice of how our enemies move
against our friends?

ISMENE
                    No word have I had,
good or bad, since we two sisters have lost
two brothers who died at the same hour, each
by the other's hand. And the Argive army fled
in the night. But beyond that, nothing
that either helps or hurts my sorry fortune.

ANTIGONE
So I assumed, which is why I called you here
outside the courtyard gates, to speak in private.

ISMENE
What is it? Your expression is very dark! Tell me.

ANTIGONE

You know that Creon has honored one of our brothers
in burial rites and dishonored the other.
Eteocles he has interred according to law
and custom more or less to be dignified
among the dead below. But for our other
brother, Polyneices, who fought as bravely
and died in the same combat, he has forbidden
these rites, proclaiming to all that none may cover
his corpse or lament it, and that he shall be left,
unmourned, for the carrion birds to defile and feast on.
This, they say, is the order of noble Creon
to you and me. To us! He is coming
here to proclaim it to all the people and let us know
that those who defy him will be stoned to death.
That is the new trouble. And now you can prove
who you are: good sister or coward
and disgrace to our brave ancestors.

ISMENE

But sister!
What do you think we can possibly do now,
you and I, to untie the difficult knot?

ANTIGONE

You must decide whether to share the risk.
Will you help me?

ISMENE

I'm afraid to ask. Help how?

ANTIGONE

Will you give me a hand? To bury our brother's body?

ISMENE
How can you think of a burial? It is forbidden.

ANTIGONE
I will do it, whether you help or not.
He is still my brother and yours too.

ISMENE
                                    Think
what Creon will do! It's reckless. Consider the risk.

ANTIGONE
He has no right to keep me from doing right.

ISMENE
Omoi! Think of our father and how he died,
hated, notorious—for the crimes that he himself
had brought to light. And then, with his own hands,
he blinded himself to shut out the light forever.
And then Jocasta, his mother and also his wife,
hanged herself. And our two brothers died
by each other's swords. Now you and I are left . . .
But think how our fate could be worse than any of theirs
to die that way for having defied Creon,
flouting the law and his power. We are mere women
and cannot fight against men. The laws of the state
have force behind them. We must submit and obey
even in so painful a thing as this.
I pray that the dead may forgive me and understand
that I am constrained, with no choice but to yield.
What you are proposing is beyond us.

ANTIGONE

I am not trying to persuade you. No,
even if you were willing, I would not let you
join me in this now. Be what you are.
You have made your choice, as I have made mine. I will
bury my brother, and if I die, it shall be
with honor. He is my own; I will lie with my own,
not guilty of any crime, but pious, holy.
We are dead for a long time, and to death's demands
there is no ending ever.
                              As for you,
ignore the gods if you can. Do as you like.

ISMENE

I do not ignore the laws of the gods. But I cannot
ignore the laws of the city and of men.

ANTIGONE

Take what comfort you can in that excuse.
I will go to heap up dirt for my dead brother.

ISMENE

Antigone, I am terrified for you.

ANTIGONE

Don't be. Think of yourself. I wish you well.

ISMENE

But keep it quiet at least. Let no one know,
and I promise you I will not say a word.

ANTIGONE

Broadcast it to the world. I shall hate you
if you do not proclaim this to everyone.

ISMENE
Your heart is hot as fire for chilling deeds.

ANTIGONE
I am pleasing the gods and the dead more than myself.

ISMENE
But will you? Can you? Has your strength no limit?

ANTIGONE
At least I shall find out what that limit is.

ISMENE
To try to do the impossible is wrong.

ANTIGONE
I'll hate you if you say that. And our dead brother
will hate you as well. Let me have my plan,
however rash. There is danger, but it won't be the worst
death that can take me. However much I suffer,
at least I shall know that I did not die in dishonor.

ISMENE
Do as you will. You're a fool. But a good sister.

[ISMENE exits into the palace. ANTIGONE exits to the right, in
the direction of the countryside and the battlefield. The CHORUS
of elders enters from the left.]

Parodos

CHORUS
O sun, whose fairest light
ever bathed the gates of Thebes,

you fixed the golden eye of day,
rising over Dirce's stream,
on the man who came from Argos
in dazzling armor
as he fled in fear
and you shook his bridle free.

FIRST CHORISTER
Contentiousness goaded
Polyneices on,
him of many quarrels,
to fly like a shrill eagle
on snow-white wings
that fluttered like his helmet's horsehair crest
and, bristling weapons, assault our city.

SECOND CHORISTER
Ringing round our seven gates
their sharp spears were hungry for blood
but before our gore glutted their gullets
or the god of fire's pine-fed flames
had destroyed the city's diadem
of walls and towers, he was gone,
repulsed, the clangor of war behind him now,
for Thebes had fended him off,
a fierce dragon breathing the fire of battle.

CHORUS
Zeus hates the tongues of braggarts
and seeing them swarming toward us,
arrogant, flashing gold,
he flung down his fire upon them,

to strike the first man who raced up our walls,
crowing Capanaeus.

FIRST CHORISTER
We heard his cry of triumph turn to terror's
scream as he fell in flames to the hard earth,
that firebrand now a guttering torch.

SECOND CHORISTER
The others behind him fell back, appalled
by his death and then their own in the din of battle.
The war god filled their mouths with the bitter dust
from his proud chariot's wake.

FIRST CHORISTER
Seven captains at seven gates,
and they left all their hopes and their weapons,
sacrifices to Zeus, who gives
victory's trophies . . .

SECOND CHORISTER
                              Except those two
unfortunate sons of the same mother
and father, who met face to face in rage
wielding spears against each other
in combat to share a common death.

CHORUS
Now the glory of Victory has come
to rejoice in Thebes' procession of chariots.
Let us forget our troubles and visit the temples
where Bacchus presides over the city to sing
and dance the night away to make earth tremble.

Scene I

[Enter, CREON from the palace. He mounts a raised step from
which he will speak.]

FIRST CHORISTER
But here is our new king, Creon . . .

SECOND CHORISTER
Menoeceus' son!

FIRST CHORISTER
                Whom the gods have given us.
What new plans has he devised to answer
Fate's fresh conundrums? Why has he convoked
his council of elders? What will he proclaim?

CREON
Citizens! With a heavy hand the gods
have shaken the city's foundation, but now those same
gods have steadied them and us and have restored
our fortunes. I have summoned you here, chosen
because I know your hearts have always been loyal
to Laius' throne and power. When Oedipus ruled
you trusted in him; and when Oedipus died, you were loyal
to his heirs, his children. Now they are both dead,
a double disaster on a single day,
killing and being killed, defiling, defiled.
And the power devolves to me, as a kin of their house.
      I realize that to see into any man's soul
and test the mettle of his thought and judgment,
you have to observe him in action discharging the duties
of high office. I have only contempt
for one who is cautious, keeps his mouth shut,

consults, and schemes for advantage, his or his kinfolk's.
I will look to the good of the entire city,
and I call Zeus to witness that I shall speak out
if I should ever see that ruin threatens
the safety of Thebes, and I shall take bold action.
I will never be a friend to one who means harm
to our city and its people. I value friendship,
but I turn my back on any who may imperil
the ship of state on which I serve as captain.

      These are the rules by which I live. My only
aim, believe me, is to make our city great.
I therefore proclaim my first edict
relating to the brothers, Oedipus's sons:
Eteocles, who died fighting for Thebes
and gave his life for us in the recent battle,
we shall bury with all honor, performing
the rites due to noble men who descend
below; but Polyneices, his brother, who came
from exile to assault his city, burn it
down to the ground, and drink his people's blood,
to enslave us all . . .

            I proclaim that none
shall bury him or lament or do him honor,
but his corpse shall be left for carrion birds and dogs
to foul and feed on.

            This is what I have decided,
for it would be wrong to treat in the same way
the patriot and the traitor. Those who are loyal
to the city deserve respect when they are alive
and every honor when they die.

FIRST CHORISTER
                              No one
can argue with that. If that is your pleasure, Creon,
son of Menoeceus, we shall obey.
It is surely within your power to make the laws
that apply both to the living and the dead.

CREON
                              That is my will.
See to it that no one dares disobey.

SECOND CHORISTER
Surely, such duty must fall to younger men . . .

CREON
No fear! There will be soldiers to guard the corpse.

FIRST CHORISTER
Then what is it that you want *us* to do?

CREON
That you give no aid to any who defy me.

FIRST CHORISTER
No one is foolish enough to want to die.

CREON
You take my point exactly. Hold on to your lives
with the same care as you hold on to your purses.

[Enter GUARD]

GUARD
My lord, I wish I could say I was out of breath
from running fast, but that would not be the truth.

Indeed, I have stopped many times, have thought of flight,
and my mind was full of contradictory notions.
Fool, it asked, why do you hurry so
to your sure ruin? And then it asked: dare you
delay? If someone gets there first, and Creon
already knows, how will it go for you?
So I hastened, and hesitated, and hastened again
not knowing what to do. In the end, I listened
to duty's voice and am here, to make my report,
afraid but resigned to my fate, whatever it is.

CREON
What is the trouble, man? Out with it. Speak.

GUARD
First, know this. It wasn't me. I didn't
do it or see who did it. It wasn't my fault!

CREON
Get to the point. Jump in! What in the world
do you find it so hard to tell me? Speak up, I say.

GUARD
It's . . . a terrible thing. I don't know how to begin.

CREON
Blurt it out, man, and then just . . . go away!

GUARD
Polyneices' body . . . Someone . . . It's buried.
There is . . . dust that someone has scattered over the corpse.
And then just disappeared. Without a trace.

CREON
What man would have dared?

GUARD
I have no idea.
I tell you, my lord, there was no mark on the ground
of spade or pick. No footprints, no cartwheel tracks.
The morning watch discovered it, and we went
and were shocked, as you can imagine. The body was covered
with dust to please the ghost. No dog had attacked,
no beast or carrion bird had torn the body.
We suspected one another, each man swearing
by all the gods in heaven he wasn't the one,
and each was ready to walk through fire to prove
he hadn't done it and didn't know who did.
Then one said that we had to report it to you,
and we all fell silent and stared at the ground, for we knew
he was right. But which should go? We drew
lots. I lost. And here I am, though I wish
I weren't as much as you must wish it. I'm sorry.
Nobody welcomes the bringer of bad news.

SECOND CHORISTER
My lord, as I have been thinking the matter over,
I wonder, is this an act of the gods . . . ?

CREON
                                        Be still,
before you drive me into a frenzy, old man.
The thing you say is . . . stupid. The gods did this?
Why? What god could care for this traitor's corpse?
What you suggest is offensive to heaven and me!
Would they favor a man who came to burn their temples

and their sacred altars, destroy our state and its laws?
Do the gods favor the wicked? What are you saying?
From the very beginning, I have heard the sedition,
the whispers in back alleys, have seen the shaking
heads. I know the plots and schemes! It's greed,
the love of money that drives them. And somebody bribed
somebody! It's money that ruins cities,
money that drives men from their homes, money
that corrupts the minds of the good with thoughts of evil!

[To the GUARD]
Whoever was paid to do this shall pay, I swear.
By Zeus himself I take my solemn oath!
Find who it is and bring him here, or death
will be what you wish for, strung up alive and groaning
in the pain you deserve for this dereliction of duty
or treachery or whatever it was. Whatever they paid you men,
you'll come to realize it wasn't nearly enough.

GUARD
Am I dismissed? Or may I say something?

CREON
Your words are hardly music to my ears.

GUARD
Are your ears the trouble, or is it perhaps your mind?

CREON
Your cheek is impressive. Anyway, what's the difference?

GUARD
My speech may grate on your ears, but the person who did
the deed is the one who really bothers you.

CREON
You're quite the chatterbox!

GUARD
                              I am not guilty.

CREON
So you claim, but I don't have to believe you.
You sold your honor for money!

GUARD
                              No, we didn't.
It's dreadful that you believe what isn't true.

CREON
Then find out who sold out and bring him to me.
Prove me wrong, or bear the brunt of my anger.

[Exit CREON into the palace.]

GUARD
Bring him the man? As if it were that easy.
What I won't be bringing here anymore is myself . . .
I can hardly believe I'm still a free man. Safety
is what I want. And I won't look for it here.
I thank the gods that somehow I'm still alive!

[Exit GUARD]

Ode I

FIRST CHORISTER
Many things are awesome, but none
is more awesome than man.

He ventures out
on the gray sea lashed by the winter winds,
braving cresting waves.
He plows the yielding earth
year after year with the strength of his tamed stallions.

SECOND CHORISTER
The giddy birds and scampering game
he traps in the coils of his nets,
and the fish in the sea
by his wits and patient skill he contrives to catch.
Beasts that roam the hills
he bests, and the shaggy-maned
horses and huge bulls he tames and yokes.

FIRST CHORISTER
And thought as quick as the wind, and speech
he has learned and put to use
to organize cities
and tame them, and likewise the skill to fend off weather,
deflecting the rain's arrows,
the blizzard's bite. He is the master of all
except implacable Hades' relentlessness.
Desperate maladies he cures
until death beats him at last.

SECOND CHORISTER
Great is the cunning he brings to bear
for good or for evil ends.
When he honors the gods'
laws, his city stands proud, but when he ignores them
what of his city then?

May the outlaw never find warmth at my hearth,
or presume to share the secret thoughts of my heart.

Scene II

[The GUARD returns, leading ANTIGONE.]

SECOND CHORISTER
What can this portend? How can this be?
Surely that is Antigone!

FIRST CHORISTER
                    We all
know her, the unhappy child of a most unhappy
father.

SECOND CHORISTER
                    Oedipus' daughter!

FIRST CHORISTER
                              What does this mean?

SECOND CHORISTER
It can't be you they're leading in as a captive,
who broke the laws of the king, can it?

THIRD CHORISTER
                              What folly!

GUARD
This is the one who did it! We caught her
burying the body! But where is Creon?

FIRST CHORISTER
Here, coming out of the palace just in time.

[Enter CREON]

CREON
What has happened? Just in time for what?

GUARD
Lord, there is nothing impossible. Never say never
or swear it is not true. I could not have believed
that I'd be standing here braving your anger
again but here I am—with the culprit, the girl
we caught red-handed, tending the grave out there.
I had sworn I would never come back here again,
but a satisfaction like this is beyond any other
pleasure, and here I am. No casting of lots.
I was the one they thought deserved the honor.
I turn her over to you to judge and convict,
and can walk away now with all this behind me.

CREON
But how did you take this girl? What happened?! Explain!

GUARD
Explain? She is the one. She was burying him.

CREON
Do you know what this means? You know what you're saying?

GUARD
                                                        Yes, sir!

We saw her out there, piling dust on the body,
defying your clear and explicit proclamation.

CREON
Give me all the details. What did you see?

GUARD
This is what happened. After your terrible threats,
we went back to the body and brushed off the dirt.
It was starting to rot already and was stinking,
so we went upwind and from a small hill we watched it,
keeping our eyes open and keeping each other
awake and alert. The sun climbed high in the sky
and then in the heat of midday there was a dust storm,
and the wind rose and the leaves on the trees were tossing
this way and that, coated with dust. Our eyes
were stinging from the plague the gods had sent.
When the wind died down, there she was. We could hear her
crying that keening note a bird can make
when its nest has been robbed by some larger bird or hungry
beast. That's what she sounded like when she saw the naked
corpse, and we heard the curses she called down
on those who had done it, which is to say, on us.
She poured more dust on the body and then she poured
from a well-wrought urn a triple libation of wine
to lay the ghost. We hastened at once to seize her
as clearly she was expecting us to do.
We charged her with this crime and the other one, too,
and she made no denial of any kind.
There could be no doubt, but still I was uneasy,
out of trouble myself but sorry to see
a friend in danger now. Still, if it's her or me,
I've got to think of myself and save my own skin.

CREON

[to ANTIGONE]
And you? You hang your head and stare at the ground,
but what have you to say? Do you deny it?

ANTIGONE
I don't deny a thing. I did what he said.

CREON

[to GUARD]
You are dismissed. You are free to go.

[Exit GUARD]

[to ANTIGONE]
                                            Tell me,
briefly. You heard my order forbidding this?

ANTIGONE
It had been published. Everyone knew. I knew.

CREON
And still, you did this? You dared to defy the law?

ANTIGONE
Yes, for it was not Zeus who made that law,
nor Justice who dwells with the gods below and rules
in the world of men and women. Your edict was clear
and strong, but not enough to suspend the unwritten,
unfailing laws of the gods who live forever
and whose rule, revealed to us so long ago,
is not for here and now but, like the gods,
forever. How could I face them? How could I think

to pay the penalty they'd have imposed for my fear
of a man, however powerful and proud?
That I would die, I knew—even before
your proclamation. Every one of us dies.
But if my death be sooner rather than later,
I'd count that a blessing, for I am burdened
by griefs only death can lift from my troubled heart.
I do not fear it. What I could not endure
was that Polyneices, my mother's son, should die
and remain unburied. That would have been painful
as death is not.
                    You think I'm a fool? I am
content to be called a fool by a greater fool.

FIRST CHORISTER
The girl is her father's daughter. Savage, wild,
she has no idea when or how to yield.

CREON
But the strongest will can break, as the hardest iron
tempered in fire can shatter, or spirited horses,
broken and tamed, can be led by a little bridle.
A slave should not be proud before a master.
The girl knows she is insolent. She transgresses
established laws, and then, compounding the crime,
laughs and gloats at the thought of what she has done.
Which one of us here is the man, she or I?
Which of us has the power? Who must give way?
She is my sister's child, or closer than that,
in a family tree that Zeus, god of the hearth,
has twisted so, but she and her sister shall not
escape a terrible death.

[To SERVANTS]

Go, fetch me Ismene!
She is guilty too. They have conspired together.
She is inside there, in the house, raving. The mind
proclaims its guilt when people plot in darkness.

[Glaring at ANTIGONE]
But this is worse, the brazenness, the defiance!

ANTIGONE
Kill me, then. What more do you want?

CREON

Nothing.
Now I have what I want.

ANTIGONE
Then why wait?
Do it! That would spare me having to hear
more talk. And my words must be distasteful
to you. What greater glory could I win
beyond what I earn by burying my brother?
If fear didn't shut their mouths, I am sure these men
would tell you they approve of what I have done.
A tyrant has the luxury of saying
and doing what he pleases.

CREON
Only you think that.

ANTIGONE
They think so, too, but are frightened and want to please you.

CREON
What if they didn't approve? Would you then be ashamed?

ANTIGONE
No, not for showing blood-kin reverence.

CREON
Eteocles was blood-kin, too, remember.

ANTIGONE
Yes, of the same mother, the same father.

CREON
How then can you insult his memory?

ANTIGONE
He will not bear witness or take offense.

CREON
No? If you honor his enemy—a traitor?

ANTIGONE
Polyneices was my brother. Not some slave.

CREON
He attacked the city Eteocles defended!

ANTIGONE
Even so, there are honors due the dead.

CREON
For the just and the unjust? The good and the wicked?

ANTIGONE
In the world below, who knows what was good or evil?

CREON
Enemies don't change, not even in death.

ANTIGONE
I was not born to feud but to love and to honor.

CREON
Then go to hell, and love and honor there,
but as long as I live, a woman shall not rule.

FIRST CHORISTER
But see, Ismene is coming out of the palace,
her flushed face streaming bitter tears.

[Enter ISMENE with GUARDS]

CREON
A viper skulking in my house! Bloodsucker!
I never supposed I was bringing up two plagues
to undermine my throne. What do you say?
Do you confess to this crime? Or will you pretend
to innocence and swear that you knew nothing?

ISMENE
If she will let me say so, I am guilty.

ANTIGONE
But that's not true. You refused. You haven't the right
to claim any part in what I did alone.

ISMENE
Now, in this dark hour, I am with you.
I am not ashamed to share in the punishment.

ANTIGONE
The dead and the gods who rule them know who performed
the required rite. Love is more than words.

ISMENE
Share your death with me, sister. Do not shame me.
Let my blood be his belated libation.

ANTIGONE
Do not claim what is not yours by right.
The deed was my own. My death will be sufficient.

ISMENE
What longing for life do I have, if you are gone?

ANTIGONE
Ask Creon, to whose decrees you give such deference.

ISMENE
Why are you so cruel? What good does it do you?

ANTIGONE
You're right. It gives me pain to say harsh things.

ISMENE
                                        Sister,
what can I do to help you?

ANTIGONE
                              Save yourself!
I want you to escape.

ISMENE
                    I am cut off.

ANTIGONE
Yes, because you chose life. I chose death.

ISMENE
I tried to tell you . . . I warned you what could happen.

ANTIGONE
Some will think you were right and others not.

ISMENE
But here we are, both in the same mess.

ANTIGONE
But you are alive. My life has long been over.
I was already dead, and I served the dead.

CREON

[To the CHORUS]
One was always mad, from the day she was born.
The other one, it appears, has just gone crazy.

ISMENE
You are right, my lord. But one does not leave one's senses.
What happens is that they depart on their own.

CREON
That may be true for you. You assumed her guilt.

ISMENE
How can I live alone and without her?

CREON
You're doing it now. She is already dead.

ISMENE
But will you put to death your own son's bride?

CREON
He can find other furrows that he can plow.

ISMENE
There was a political rightness to the match.

CREON
I want no evil woman for my son's wife.

ISMENE
Poor Haemon! How your father wrongs you.

CREON
Not another word about marriages!

ISMENE
Creon, will you take Antigone from him?

CREON
Hades will prevent the marriage, not me.

ISMENE
She really is to die, then?

CREON
                          It's settled, and you and I
both know it.

[to the GUARDS]
                          Take them inside at once,
and keep close watch, for even brave men run
in the face of death, and these are only women.

[The GUARDS take ANTIGONE and ISMENE into the palace.]

Ode II

FIRST CHORISTER
Happy are they who have never been touched by evil.
For those whom the gods afflict, shaking their houses,
disaster impends. It swells like a raging sea
when the water is black and bitter winds from Thrace
lash it in fury to roil the dark sands and beat
      loud on the suffering shore.

SECOND CHORISTER
I have seen this ancient sorrow looming
that strikes Oedipus' house, unsated, unspent,
from generation to generation: the gods
do not relent or abate their divine rage.
This last blossom of Labdacus' noble line
      opened briefly in sunlight.

CHORUS

[Alternating sentences or, if they can manage it, in unison.]
But the underworld gods and the fates are cutting it down
in their anger at intemperate words and actions.
What mortal can stand up to Zeus whose power time
cannot sap, whom sleep can never gentle?
It is always dazzling day in his house on Olympus.
      Present, future, and past

shimmer together: the laws of the gods are timeless,
one of which is that often to wealth and great power

catastrophe comes. Men may dream of profit
but they walk as blind men walk, straight into the fire.
When the gods drive men to disaster, evil seems good.
We keep our heads down.

Scene III

FIRST CHORISTER
But here comes Haemon, your youngest son.

SECOND CHORISTER
Is he angry about Antigone's fate? Or grieving?

[Enter HAEMON, from stage left]

CREON
There's no need to guess. We'll know soon enough.

[To HAEMON]

My son,
you have no doubt heard my judgment about that girl.
Do you come here in hate and rebellion, or is it in love
and deference to your father, no matter what?

HAEMON
You are my father and my guide, and I belong
to you and always defer to your good judgment.
No marriage could mean more to me than your wisdom.

CREON
Excellent, son. That's how it ought to be.
You should give way to your father's judgment. This
is what men hope and pray for, that they may beget

and rear in their households offspring who do them honor,
obedient and loyal, their enemies' foe,
their friends' friend. Of the man who fathers rebellious
children who do not help him, what can one say?
He has begotten trouble for himself
and joy to those who hate him!
Never let go of your good sense, my son,
certainly not for the pleasure a woman can give you,
all too often a troublesome armful that turns
cold soon enough—and there you are with an evil
woman beside you in your bed and sharing your hearth.
Loveless love? It is an incurable wound!
Hawk and spit her out. Let her find a husband
in Hades! I caught her, the only one in the city
to disobey my law. She has to die.
Let her invoke Zeus, the god of kindred,
but I cannot shrink from the duty I owe the city.
If my own relative disregards the law,
what can I expect from anyone else?
It is only a man who can keep his own house in order
whom anyone ought to trust to rule the city.
Insubordination? Rebelliousness?
These are the ruin not only of family life
but of government as well. A leader must be
respected, obeyed in all things, right or wrong.
Only the man who knows how to obey
can understand what it is to command and give orders
when the spears are coming at him and his time
to lead has come. It's discipline that counts.
But if we are to lose, at least let it be
at the hand of a man. If you're going to be defeated
by a woman, who is weaker—that's a disgrace.

SECOND CHORISTER
Unless we have gone senile, what you say
about these matters seems to make perfect sense.

HAEMON
Father, the greatest gift the gods have given
men is the light of reason, and I can see
that what you say is right. For me to disagree
would be to cast away that precious possession.
And yet among many men there will be many
different opinions. Some of these can be helpful,
and no one, not even you, can know their minds.
I'm not the one to say you are in error,
but there may be some who disagree.
And you cannot know—it is not in your nature—
what they may say or do, or whom they blame.
Because of who you are, they are afraid
to tell you what you may not like to hear.
But I am less formidable, and I hear
what they are thinking and saying under their breath
or even aloud, lamenting for this girl.
The talk is how no woman has ever deserved
less to suffer so miserable a death.
What she did was a generous, pious action.
She buried her brother? Was this a shameful deed?
For this, ought she to be punished or given honor?
That is what they are saying, and I report it
as a dutiful son should do, for nothing means more
to me than that you should prosper and rule securely
and well. For you to be held in the highest repute
is what I desire, as any son would want
for his father or any father would want for his son.

Do not be too constrained in this but consider
other opinions and other possible choices.
The man whose cast of mind binds him too tightly
so that he thinks that he alone is right
and everyone else is always wrong . . . he runs
a terrible risk. The wise are willing to learn
and not to resist correction—like trees in a storm
that yield to the winds and the waters and survive,
while those that are rigid, no matter how large they be,
fall, their branches, trunks, and even their roots
overturned. The sailor who keeps the sheet
too taut in a gale will turn turtle, his boat
and oarsmen lost. Retreat from your anger, father.
Young as I am, I have some judgment, I think,
and I say wisdom ought to acknowledge its limits.
Anyone can make mistakes. What's wise
is to know how and when to accept correction.

FIRST CHORISTER
Lord, if what he says is worth listening to,
listen, as you, Haemon, should to your father.

CREON
A man of my age should be schooled by a stripling youth?

HAEMON
I'm speaking of justice. It is not my age that matters,
but what I say and do.

CREON
                              Is it right to do
honor to traitors? Is that what you advocate?!

HAEMON
Not at all. I don't defend evildoers

CREON
But what about her? Has she not committed a crime?

HAEMON
The people of Thebes don't think so, no.

CREON
Do the people of Thebes rule me? Or do I rule them?

HAEMON
Which of us now sounds like a petulant youth?

CREON
However I sound, I'm the one giving orders!

HAEMON
What city takes its orders from a single man?

CREON
The people of this city are all my subjects.

HAEMON
If you can't stand dissent, go rule in a desert!

CREON

[speaking to the CHORUS]
The boy has sold out to a woman. He's taken her side.

HAEMON
Are you a woman, then? It's your side I'm taking.

CREON
You brawl in public with me? It's for my sake?

HAEMON
I'm trying to mediate in your brawl with justice.

CREON
Justice? I'm in the right, and within my rights.

HAEMON
Your rights end where the rights of the gods begin.

CREON
Villain! Worse than a woman. The slave of a woman!

HAEMON
                                        No, sir!
I simply refuse to agree to what is shameful!

CREON
Every word you speak is in her behalf.

HAEMON
I speak for you and me, and the gods below.

CREON
You will never marry that girl while she is alive.

HAEMON
Then she must die. But she shall not die alone.

CREON
What? You think you can threaten me that way?

HAEMON

It isn't a threat. I'm telling you what I've decided.

CREON

You'll regret all this. I think you are out of your mind.

HAEMON

If you weren't my father, I'd say *you* were crazy.

CREON

Never mind "father!" You are the lunatic now.

HAEMON

There's just no talking to you. You refuse to listen.

CREON

I hear every word you say, and I swear by Olympus
you shall not continue these insults and expect
my continuing forbearance.

[To the SERVANTS]
                                        Bring out the girl.
Let him watch the despicable creature die
before her darling bridegroom's horrified eyes!

HAEMON

It won't happen. And you won't see me again.
Rave on, as long as anyone's willing to listen.

                              [Exit HAEMON to the left]

FIRST CHORISTER

My lord, he's gone. Just as he said. And the temper
of a young man of that age . . . ? Who knows what he'll do?

CREON
Let him do whatever his pride prompts,
but he cannot save those girls from death.

FIRST CHORISTER
                                    Those girls?
You plan to kill both of them?

CREON
                                    No, you're right.
Not the one who did not touch the corpse.

SECOND CHORISTER
And the one who did? What death do you plan for her?

CREON
There's a remote path nobody uses,
and out there is a cave. I'll wall her in
with just enough food and water to keep the city
free of a murder's pollution. There she can pray
to Hades—the only god she seems to revere.
Let Hades show her a way to escape—or else
teach her that all her piety is useless.

[Exit CREON into the palace.]

Ode III

FIRST CHORISTER
Love, invincible,
Love, who can ruin the richest man, tempting
with sweet nights by the soft cheeks of a girl,
you range over the seas and into remote

woodsmen's huts. Not even the immortal
gods can escape you.
Mortals, in our brief
stays in the sunlight, you seize
and drive us mad.

SECOND CHORISTER
The judicious man you craze
and the orderly mind you unhinge.
See how you have kindled intemperate rage
between father and son,
both of them victims and losers
before your awful power.
A girl's glance is a thunderbolt from above,
from the merciless playfulness of Aphrodite.

Scene IV

[ANTIGONE is led in by GUARDS]

FIRST CHORISTER
There is in my heart, at seeing this, rebellion,
and I can barely restrain the stream of tears
that wells up at the sight of Antigone's passing
before us to that soporific bed
to which at the end of the day we all must go.

ANTIGONE
Look at me, fellow townsmen, and have pity
as I take my last walk in the light of the sun
that will no longer shine upon me. Lulling Death
beckons me, still living, to Acheron's shore

in dismal stillness. No wedding music will play
as that stern bridegroom takes me for his own.

SECOND CHORISTER
You go in honor and strength and your full beauty,
admired by all. No diminution by sickness
or disfiguring wounds of battle will have touched you.
Of your own free will you make your stately descent.

ANTIGONE
I had heard Niobe's story, Tantalus' daughter,
and thought it was the saddest death there could be,
in the stone's embrace near Sipylus' heights, in the endless rain
and the silent snow where, with ever-weeping eyes,
she bedews her mountain ridge. Her grief is mine.

FIRST CHORISTER
But she was born of the gods, and we are mortals,
the children of mortals. To achieve such a godlike fate
has a glory in it, in this world and the next.

ANTIGONE
You mock me? At such a moment, you insult me?
In the name of my fathers' gods, why? I am still
here, alive. Can't you wait till I'm dead?
O, my splendid city! O, Dirce's fountains!
I call upon you to witness how I am treated
by these prosperous men with chariots and fine horses
as I make my way to the home in the hollow rock
where the laws of Thebes have sent me. How very strange,
I am no longer living but not yet dead, and I float
in misery between the two different worlds.

SECOND CHORISTER
You have braved all human limits and now confront
the lofty altar of Justice. Poor suffering girl!
You are punished perhaps for the crimes of your famous father.

ANTIGONE
It may well be. I think of that bridal bed
in pity and terror. Oedipus, father and brother,
he did not know, and his catastrophe
has involved us all in Labdacus' noble house.
That coupling with our mother was punishment
and crime at the same time, and we are the issue,
misery's heirs. I go to join them now,
unmarried and accursed. Polyneices married.
His wedding gift was the Argive army that killed him,
and now will kill me, too.

FIRST CHORISTER
The respect you showed
your brother is noble indeed, but you did not give
the same respect to power. And in your passion
and willfulness, I fear you are destroyed.

ANTIGONE
No tears for me, no friends, no strain of music,
no bridal song but only funeral dirge
as I make my way along this unhappy road
in the last of the light I shall ever see. The sacred
eye of the sun will close upon me forever.

[Enter CREON and ATTENDANTS through the central door of
the palace.]

CREON

Wailing? Complaining? It won't make any difference
or postpone death for even a moment. Why
do people bother? Take her away at once.
And when she is stowed in that tomb, as I have ordered,
leave her there to do whatever she pleases—
live or die. It has nothing to do with us.
Above ground we are rid of her. And guiltless.

ANTIGONE

In a cold tomb, on a wedding bed of rock
I shall be with my people again, where Queen
Persephone rules the numberless ghosts of the dead.
The saddest arrival, come before my time,
I shall see my father, my dear mother, and you,
Polyneices, whose body these hands lately washed
and for whom I poured the proper libations. And this
is my reward. I think wise men would say
that what I did was right to honor you
in the way I did and therefore that Creon was wrong.
Had it been my children or my husband
moldering out there, I could have married
another man. Or had another child.
But my mother and father are dead, and there was no other
brother who could take your place. For your sake
I did what I did, to do you honor. This,
Creon says, was recklessness, and he leads me
thus by the hand, without a marriage, without
children, or friends, alive, to the house of the dead.
What law of the gods have I broken? Obedient
to them I am condemned. If I have been wrong,
I forgive my judge, but if what I did was right,

may the gods punish him who condemns me. Let
his suffering be equal to my own.

FIRST CHORISTER
The blasts of those harsh winds still buffet her heart.

CREON
The guards shall have cause to regret their lack of dispatch.

ANTIGONE
His voice is like the voice of death itself.

CREON
Your nice turn of phrase, I regret to say, is correct.

ANTIGONE
City of Thebes and gods of my forefathers,
see how I am led away, the last
of a royal house. See what I suffer from men
for having shown the laws of heaven reverence.

[ANTIGONE, guarded, exits right.]

Ode IV

FIRST CHORISTER
Danaë, too, was locked away
imprisoned in a cell small as a tomb,
and she, too, came of a noble house.
But Zeus came down to her in a golden shower.
Oh, my poor child,
the power of Fate is strange and very strong.
Neither wealth nor martial valor can stand against it.

The sturdiest of ships cannot prevail
against its crashing waves.

SECOND CHORISTER
Think also of Dryas' son,
Lycurgus. The god sealed him up in a rocky fastness,
for he had defied the power of Dionysos,
a mad king to contend against divine
madness. He learned, too late,
not to mock the revels, not to offend
the inspired women, the dancing, the Bacchanalian
music of the night, the sound of the pipes
that resonates in the darkness.

FIRST CHORISTER
By the Bosporus' shore,
in Thrace where the neck of land divides the two
seas, at Salmydessus, Ares watched
while Phineus' crazed wife,
Eidothea, blinded his two sons, plunging
the loom's shuttles into their orbs
weaving blood and darkness.

SECOND CHORISTER
They wept for their wounds,
and their mother, Phineus' first wife,
whom their father had locked away,
Boreas' daughter, raised in his faraway caves.
Even to her, a child of a god, the Fates
were harsh. My child,
noble blood can't help.

Scene V

[Enter TIRESIAS, blind, led by a BOY, from the left.]

TIRESIAS
Lords of Thebes, the two of us have come here
with the one pair of eyes. Thus, the blind cope.

CREON
Tiresias, old sir, what brings you here?

TIRESIAS
I am the soothsayer, and I will say.

CREON
And I will listen, as I have always done.

TIRESIAS
Which is how you have steered the city and kept it on course.

CREON
You have been helpful always, and I am grateful.

TIRESIAS
Then listen. And think. Your fate hangs in the balance.

CREON
That has an ominous sound. What is the matter?

TIRESIAS
I tell you this, as my arcane arts have prompted.
I took my usual place where the birds instruct,
and where I can read their signs and omens, and heard
a strange sound, as they screeched with a sudden frenzy.
They were going at one another with bloody claws

as the furious whirring of wings above my head
made all too clear. I admit that I was frightened,
and I tried to offer a sacrifice, but the god
would not allow the flame to rise from the altar.
The embers died down, and a slime oozed from the thigh-bone
to sputter in clouds of acrid smoke, and bitter
gall sprayed into the air. The wrappings of fat
deliquesced. The rite was a disaster.
The boy described it all, as I, in turn,
interpret for you the dire meaning. You
have brought this plague upon the city. Our altars
are covered with foul bits the dogs and birds
have brought from Polyneices' rotting corpse.
The gods, disgusted, no longer hear our prayers.
And the birds are driven crazy having feasted
on the clotted blood of the body you left for them.

      My son, consider this. Men make mistakes.
Everyone does. But some retrieve and recoup,
correcting their errors—unless they are stubborn and proud.
Be willing to take the good advice I offer.
Don't be a fool! The man out there is dead,
and you keep stabbing at him . . . What is the point?
Where is the honor in that? Heed these words
I offer for your welfare and your profit!

CREON
What am I? Some kind of bull's-eye for your arrows?
You and your profiteer prophets, what are you after,
telling me what to do? Power? Money?
Even if eagles swooped down on that body
and carried its rotting bits up to the throne
of Zeus himself, you would not bury him.

What mortals do cannot defile the gods.
Leave me alone. Do not try to meddle
in how I run the city. If you can read
the future, go into business, speculate,
import gold from Sardis, buy and sell,
make money—how can you miss?—on every deal.

TIRESIAS
Creon, Creon, you do not understand . . .

CREON
More sooth, for heaven's sake? Well, go ahead.

TIRESIAS
Wisdom is a greater treasure than treasure.

CREON
And foolishness is worse than any disease.

TIRESIAS
That's what you have, and a very serious case.

CREON
I dislike speaking rudely to a prophet.

TIRESIAS
You want to tell me politely that I am wrong?

CREON
There are some prophets in it for the money.

TIRESIAS
And many rulers who turn out to be corrupt.

CREON
But rulers you nag at have guards and soldiers.

TIRESIAS
It was with my help that you saved the city.

CREON
You were useful once. Not any more.

TIRESIAS
You provoke me into telling unpleasant secrets.

CREON
Something someone paid you to say to me?

TIRESIAS
Can you truly think that that is why I came here?

CREON
Whyever you came, I'm not changing my mind.

TIRESIAS
Then hear me, Creon. You shall not see the sun
make many circuits before you have to pay
corpse for corpse for those you have dishonored:
a dead man's body left unburied, defiled
and therefore defiling; a live girl put in a tomb.
You do not rule over life and death. You cannot
keep here what belongs to the gods below,
a corpse, unburied, obscene. Or send the living
into a tomb. And the gods resent your intrusion
into their domain. Therefore will Furies
attend you, relentless avengers dispatched from Hades,
to ensnare you in those nets you yourself have woven.

You think I have been bribed to say these things?
Can you buy me off for money? In your household men
and women will weep, and in other distant cities
whose sons' bodies rot before Thebes' gates
and are torn apart by dogs or carrion birds
wafting their stink to the city and its hearths,
there will be hatred and curses upon your head.
These are my arrows. You shall feel their sting.

                                                [To the BOY]
Lead me homeward, lad. Let him vent
his anger on younger men, or learn to sharpen
his mind or keep control of his too sharp tongue.

[Exit TIRESIAS.]

FIRST CHORISTER
My lord, my lord! He's gone. Not since my black
hair grew in and then turned snowy white,
not in all that time have I heard him speak
falsely to the city. What fearful words!

CREON
What can I do? I am uncertain, unsure . . .
To yield to him would be terrible, but to resist,
to disregard what he says . . . That could be worse.

SECOND CHORISTER
Wise men always know when to take advice.

CREON
Tell me what to do. I will obey.

FIRST CHORISTER
Go to the tomb. Release the living girl.
And put into it the body of the brother.

CREON
Is that what you think? That I should back off? Give way?

SECOND CHORISTER
Yes, and without delay. The vengeance of gods
is swift. You must act quickly to avoid it.

CREON
It's hard. But I shall swallow my pride, yield
to necessity, and do what I have to do.

FIRST CHORISTER
Then do it. Don't order it done but do it yourself.

CREON
I will. Right now.

[To his SERVANTS]
Assemble the guards. Get picks
and shovels, and let us go to that cave to release her.
I'll be there, myself. I was the one who did this
and now that I've changed my mind, I must make it right.
There's no getting away from the old traditions,
their safety, their wisdom. That is the way to live.

[Exit CREON.]

Paean

FIRST CHORISTER
O Semele's child, and son of Thunderer Zeus,
god of many names,
Italy's lord and ruler of the plain
of welcoming Demeter's Eleusis,
you dwell with us in Thebes, the mother city
of the mad Bacchantes,
here where Ismenos flows,
where Cadmus sowed the dragon's teeth
to bring forth soldiers.

SECOND CHORISTER
By the smoky flames of the torches worshipers carry
we can see the heights of Delphi
on the looming twin-peaked mountain.
Its Castalian Stream knows you well
where the nymphs emerge from their caves to perform your dances.
The vineyard slopes
of Nysa across on Euboea
echo their cry, *Evohé, Evohé!*
O Lord, hear our prayer!

FIRST CHORISTER
You honor Thebes above all cities
as your mother did, too, whom the lightning struck.
Now that plague threatens,
come to us, with your cleansing footsteps
descend from Parnassus
or rise up from the blue sea.

SECOND CHORISTER
We pray, we implore you, protect us,
you who lead the dance of the wheeling stars,
shepherd of dark voices,
son of Zeus, appear to us,
with your Maenad throng,
Iacchus, lord of rapture.

Exodos

[Enter MESSENGER]

MESSENGER
Men of Cadmus' city, you who dwell
within Amphion's walls . . .
                              Who can tell about life
as it goes along, lucky or catastrophic,
and always changing, so that the high and low
are always at risk, and no one can say what will happen,
or how or when or to whom. Creon, for instance,
he was the lord of the city, respected, admired.
He had saved our land from its enemies. He was monarch
and guide, with a noble brace of sons, and happy
if any man was happy.
                        And now? It's gone,
it's all gone, every source of joy
or satisfaction taken away. He has nothing
left to live for. He is a corpse still able
to walk around but not understanding why.
Wealth and power? Position? What do they mean
if the soul of the man who has them has gone up in smoke?

FIRST CHORISTER
What is this new grief for the royal house?

MESSENGER
They are dead. And those who are left alive are guilty.

SECOND CHORISTER
Who is the murderer? Who is dead? Tell us!

MESSENGER
Haemon is dead. A hemorrhage, one might say.

FIRST CHORISTER
What in the world are you talking about? Did Creon kill him?

MESSENGER
He stabbed himself—in anger against his father.

SECOND CHORISTER
What Tiresias said turns out to have been correct.

MESSENGER
That is one possible way to read it.

[Enter EURYDICE, from the center doors with ATTENDANTS.]

FIRST CHORISTER

[Sotto voce, to SECOND CHORISTER]
It's Eurydice, Creon's wife!

SECOND CHORISTER

[Also sotto voce.]
                              Do you think she heard?

EURYDICE
Citizens, all of you. Yes, I heard the news.
Or overheard. As I was about to leave
to pray to Athena for help and was sliding the bolt,
I heard your words of disaster, and the bolts
of my ears and my heart shot shut. And of my mouth.
Struck dumb, I collapsed then into the arms
of my serving women. But tell me again, clearly
and honestly, what happened? I am inured
to terrible news.

MESSENGER
                              I was there, my lady,
and I will tell it all, the whole ugly truth,
for there is no point in my trying to soothe or be gentle.
You'd learn what happened, and then you'd hate me for lying.
The truth is always better.
                              I went with your husband
to the edge of the plain where Polyneices' corpse
still lay, unpitied, torn by the foraging dogs.
We recited payers to Hecate, goddess of crossroads,
and to Pluto, too, for mercy and forgiveness.
We washed the body with purifying water
and gathered fresh branches to make a pyre
and burn the remains of the remains. Over
the urn we heaped up a burial mound
of the earth of his own city.
                              When we were done,
we ran to the girl's bridal vault and her couch
of cold stone, and as we approached we heard
a loud wail that came from inside the chamber.
Then Creon arrived. He heard it too, that cry

that floated around us indistinct but clearly
woeful. And Creon answered it with a groan
and said, "I fear I am a prophet," and then,
"How can I walk this saddest of all paths
I have ever traveled? It is my son's voice!"
He asked us to hurry and help him, and he ordered
someone to crawl in through the gap in the stones
the work crew had made and say if the gods deceived him
or it was indeed his son Haemon's voice.
We made our way into the cave and saw
at the far end of the chamber the girl, hanging.
She'd made the noose of strips of her linen clothing,
and he was there too, Haemon, his arms
around her waist, weeping, weeping, weeping
for the girl, his loss, their ruin, this terrible union
that ought to have been a marriage. Creon came in,
saw them, and with a dreadful groan cried out,
"How could you do this? Had you lost your mind?
What were you thinking?" And then, to Haemon: "My son,
my son, come out, as a suppliant I beg you!"
But Haemon only glared with eyes alight
in fury, and then he spat in his father's face.
That was when he drew his two-edged sword,
and the father drew back as the son lunged and missed,
and then, in his anger with himself, he turned
the blade and embraced it, driving it half its length
into his own side. And still alive,
he clasped the girl in the crook of his arm while his blood
spurted out, a crimson jet that sprayed
her alabaster cheek. Then he collapsed,
a corpse embracing a corpse, having achieved

the marriage rite that had been denied the couple,
together at last in Hades' gloomy house.

[Slowly, EURYDICE turns and exits into the palace.]

FIRST CHORISTER
Not a word, neither good nor bad.

SECOND CHORISTER
                                        Just gone.

MESSENGER
It's not a good sign. Perhaps her grief
is too great for her to put on show in public.
Maybe she prefers to be by herself
to mourn her son. She is a sensible woman.
She won't do anything foolish.

SECOND CHORISTER
                                        I hope not,
but I'm afraid of what might happen in there.

MESSENGER
You're right. She shouldn't be left alone. I'll go.
You never can be sure what people may do.

[Exit MESSENGER into the palace. Almost immediately, CREON
enters, with attendants. He is carrying HAEMON's body.].

FIRST CHORISTER
The lord approaches, bearing in his arms
his heavy burden, a demonstration to all
of what a man's madness can do to him.
The error was his, and the consequence is . . .

SECOND CHORISTER

Grave?

CREON

Ohhhhhh!!

For my mistakes, my obstinacy . . .

It was life and death, and I chose wrong. Look

at a father and son, who have done and suffered murder!

Ohhhhh!

The terrible decisions that I made.

My son, my son, you fled from me and from life.

And it was my fault, my own grievous fault.

FIRST CHORISTER

You come to your senses now, but it's too late.

CREON

Omoi!

How have I learned, and how unhappy I am,

and the gods have sent down upon me this great weight

of my disaster. They nudged me down the path

of savagery, and all my joys are vanished.

Ohhhhh! Ohhhhh!

Alas, alas, for the bitter troubles of men!

[Enter SECOND MESSENGER.]

MESSENGER

My lord, you carry this sorrow in your arms,

but there is more in the house that you will discover.

CREON

After this, what matters? What could be worse?

MESSENGER
Your wife, that unhappy woman, the mother of this
dead boy . . . has joined him. She is dead.

CREON
Ohhhhh! Ohhhh!
Greedy Hades, never satisfied.
Why do you destroy me?

[CREON puts the body of HAEMON down on a bier, then turns
and speaks to the MESSENGER.]
And you! You bring me this terrible news? What is this?
I was a dead man, and you kill me again.
What are you saying, lad? Aieee! Aieee!
Death upon death!

[The great door opens, and the body of EURYDICE is revealed.]

MESSENGER
Look, my lord, you can see with your own eyes.

CREON
Evil on evil! Evil on evil.
A moment ago, I had my dead son in my arms.
And now, there is my wife. Weep, weep,
for the mother in such torment for her son.

MESSENGER
She died at the altar. A thrust of a sharp sword
closed her darkening eyes, lamenting still for Megareus,
her elder son who died, and now for Haemon,
and she called down her curses on you, killer of sons.

CREON
Aieee! Aieee!
My mind turns cartwheels of fear! Someone help me,
come to me with a two-edged sword and strike
my miserable heart. I drown in woe.

MESSENGER
She was as bitter in her accusations
of your guilt for her sons' deaths as well as her own.

CREON
Tell me, how did she kill herself?

MESSENGER
She stabbed herself in the guts, to feel the pain
she knew her son had felt, and draw it out.

CREON
Omoi! Ohhhh! The grief is mine as the fault
was all mine. I was the one. I killed them,
poor mother and poor son. It's true.
Take me away, I beg of you. Take me away
quickly. I do not exist. I am less than nothing.

FIRST CHORISTER
That's good, if suffering ever does any good.
Drawing it out will only make it more painful.

CREON
Let it come, let it come.
The quickest death is best. Let it come now.
This is my last day. I never want
to see another.

SECOND CHORISTER
The days to come are the business of someone else.
Today's griefs and tasks are more than sufficient.

CREON
All I want is the end that I have prayed for.

FIRST CHORISTER
Prayers? At this point, Fate has taken over.

CREON
I don't know which way to look, at him or at her.
Everything I have touched has turned out badly.
And my fate breaks on my head and pounds me down.

[Exit CREON with his attendants.]

FIRST CHORISTER
What can you say? Wisdom is what you need.

SECOND CHORISTER
And piety toward the gods. You need that too.

FIRST CHORISTER
And never, never boast. That's dangerous.

SECOND CHORISTER
Some of us, by the time we get to be old,
have learned at least a little.

FIRST CHORISTER
                              But it's never enough.

[The CHORUS, muttering unintelligibly to each other, exits left,
toward the city.]

Oedipus Tyrannos

Dramatis Personae

OEDIPUS	tyrant of Thebes
JOCASTA	his wife
CREON	his brother-in-law
TIRESIAS	the blind prophet of Apollo
CHORUS	of elders of Thebes
A PRIEST	
FIRST MESSENGER	
SECOND MESSENGER	
A HERDSMAN	

Silent Roles

BOY	Tiresias's guide
ANTIGONE	daughter of Oedipus and Jocasta
ISMENE	daughter of Oedipus and Jocasta

Prologue

[The gateway of the palace of Oedipus in Thebes. There are altars, right and left. A group of SUPPLIANTS has come with branches of olive leaves in which strands of wool have been twined, and among these is a PRIEST. From the central door that leads into the palace, OEDIPUS enters.]

OEDIPUS
My children, the latest to spring from Cadmus' stock,
why do you sit before my house with your votive
garlands? The whole city is filled with wailing,
lamentations, and prayers to Apollo. Incense
fills the air. I have not sent to inquire
but have come myself to hear from you directly,
I, Oedipus, whom all call famous.

[To the PRIEST]
                                    You, sir,
as a priest and elder, you are a fitting spokesman.
Say what the people fear or what they desire.
What can I do to be helpful in any way?
I am not hard of heart and cannot but feel
pity in the face of such supplication.

PRIEST
Oedipus, ruler of our country, see
how we all assemble here at your altars, the fledgling
young, others, like me, a priest of Zeus,
bowed down with age, and others still who are chosen
from among the unmarried youth, with our olive chaplets
here and in the agora, at Athena's

shrine, and at the temple, too, where Ismenus
interprets the tongues of fire.

                    The city, storm-tossed,
cannot lift her prow from beneath the killing
waves. The buds are blighted and do not ripen
to fruit, the cattle are blighted too, and our women
birth dead babies. The god who carries fire
has visited us with fevered pestilence
to harry the house of Cadmus and all Thebes.
Black Pluto reaps a treasure of groans and tears.

      We do not come to this altar as suppliants
to a god but to you as the first man of the city,
wise in the ways of the world and even conversant
with higher powers, for you were the one who saved us,
putting an end to the cruel songs of the Sphinx
and the terrible toll she exacted. This you accomplished
without any help from any of us, who had no
instruction or lore to offer. It was by your own
wit and strength, god-given, that you then set
our lives aright. And now we come again,
to implore your help and beg for your protection
whether through mortal shrewdness or heavenly prompting.
In such times of trouble, men who consult together
have a better chance of survival. O best of men,
rescue the city, raise us up. We look
to you who are famous for your zeal years ago.
Let your reign not be any mockery
of a rescue that only postponed our ruin. Save us
and keep us. Let that other occasion be
an omen of a good outcome yet again.
You are our ruler and cannot wish to preside

over an empty city of death and silence,
sorry as some ghost ship or abandoned dwelling.

OEDIPUS
I pity you, my children, and know your sorrows
and why you have come. I understand there is sickness,
but none is as sick as I am. You each feel pain
alone, but I feel all your pains together,
and my soul cries out for myself and all of Thebes.
You have not aroused me from a sleep,
for I have been ruminating about this, weeping
and wandering many winding roads of thought.
One remedy have I found, and this I've applied,
sending Creon, Menoeceus' son,
my wife's brother, to consult in the Pythian hall
of Phoebus Apollo at Delphi and ask by what
word or deed I may heal and protect the city.
I have counted the days since he left and am concerned,
wondering how he has fared. He should by now
have returned. But I assure you, when he arrives,
may I myself turn out to be the villain
if I do not take what action the god has prescribed.

PRIEST
Your words are reassuring—and opportune,
for men even now are signaling Creon's approach.

OEDIPUS
I pray to Apollo that he may come bright-eyed,
his face alight with the knowledge we all require.

PRIEST
I can see that his head is crowned with a wreath
of laurel leaves, so he may be bringing comfort.

OEDIPUS
We'll find out soon enough. He is within
hailing distance.

[Enter CREON.]
Creon, my brother-in-law, Menoeceus' son,
what news have you come to bring us from the god?

CREON
Good news! I'd say that our troubles are hard to bear,
but if one can see an end to them, that's good.

OEDIPUS
What is the message, exactly? It is hard to tell
how the balance tilts between our worries and hopes.

CREON
Shall I tell you here, in front of the people? I can.
Or would you prefer that we go inside to talk?

OEDIPUS
Speak out and let them all hear it as soon as I do.
I lament for them as much as for myself.

CREON
I will report then what I heard from the god.
Lord Apollo orders us in plain words
to drive from our land the source of its pollution,
one that the country has nourished. This defilement
we can feed no more until it is destroyed.

OEDIPUS
What defilement? And how do we purify?

CREON
The purification is banishment. The foulness
is bloodshed, which must be repaid with blood.
The winds of that guilt have been battering our city.

OEDIPUS
Whose murder? What man's fate does the god reveal?

CREON
My lord, it is Laius, who was lord before you came.

OEDIPUS
I've heard of him, of course, but I never saw him.

CREON
The god was clear: he was killed; his killers
have to be punished—whoever they may be.

OEDIPUS
But where are they? Where shall such an ancient
and faint track of guilt be found and followed?

CREON
Here, in this country, he said. And we must find it
or else whoever it was could get away.

OEDIPUS
Where was it that Laius met his bloody end?
In his house? In the fields? Or in some other country?

CREON
Laius left the city and was on his way
to Delphi, or so he said. He never came home.

OEDIPUS
Surely there were servants, attendants . . . Did no
companion survive who could report what happened?

CREON
They were all killed but one, who ran away,
and could say nothing for certain—except one thing.

OEDIPUS
One clue might lead to another. At least it's a place
for us to start. What did he say?

CREON
                                        That they met
with a band of robbers. It wasn't one man's strength
that killed them all but the hands of many men.

OEDIPUS
How could the robbers dare assault the king?
Unless it was a plot and somebody paid them . . .

CREON
There were some who thought that, but in those troubled times,
we never found out or made any progress at all.

OEDIPUS
Troubled times? The king had been killed. What greater
trouble could have interfered with your search?

CREON
That was the time of the Sphinx, her terrible riddle,
and the tribute she demanded. We were dealing with that.

OEDIPUS
I shall begin again, and into that darkness
cast what light is needed, for Phoebus is right,
and you are also right to be concerned
about the death of that man. It calls out for justice
for his sake and the country's and the gods'
so that you will look upon me as an ally.
It is not an abstract duty that impels me,
but I act in my own interest driving away
this source of pollution. Whoever killed him could turn
his violence in my direction. I act
to defend him but I also defend myself.
      Come then, my children, rise from these steps, take up
these boughs of supplication and leave these altars.
We shall call another assembly now
of the people of Cadmus' city to let them know
that I shall take every possible measure in this
endeavor, and, with the help of the gods, succeed
as we must—for otherwise we shall all perish.

PRIEST
Arise, children. What he has promised us
is what we came to ask for. May Phoebus Apollo
who sent these prophecies help us end this plague.

[The PRIEST and the SUPPLIANTS exit stage right. OEDIPUS
and CREON exit into the palace through the center doors. Then the
CHORUS of Theban elders enters from the orchestra in procession.]

Parodos

FIRST CHORISTER
What is this sweet word that has
come from the gold-rich Pytho,
inspired by Zeus and Apollo,
to glorious Thebes?

SECOND CHORISTER
I am filled with terror, O god,
healer from Delos,
whom men invoke in awe
both in doubt and amazement.

THIRD CHORISTER
What will you now accomplish,
what miracle bring us,
creating or recreating,
as the seasons revolve?

CHORUS
Speak to us, earth-sustaining child
of Zeus, immortal Athena.

FIRST CHORISTER
On you I call, and your sister
Artemis, our protector,
on her throne of Fame.

SECOND CHORISTER
She presides in the marketplace.
And far-darting Apollo,
we pray to you as well
to ward off doom.

THIRD CHORISTER
In long gone ages,
when destruction loomed,
you drove ruin's flames
far from our gates.

CHORUS
Come to us now, you three, to help us again!

FIRST CHORISTER
Who can count our troubles?
The contagion spreads.
We have no means to fight it
and the land is sick.

SECOND CHORISTER
The fruits of the glorious earth
wither and die,
from the pains of women in childbirth
come tiny corpses.

THIRD CHORISTER
Swift as sparks of fire,
their souls take flight
like birds on the wing heading West,
to Hades' dark house.

CHORUS
Their deaths are beyond counting; the city is dying.

FIRST CHORISTER
Bodies, unburied, unmourned,
are strewn by the roadside.

At altars, wives and old women
groan in their grief.

SECOND CHORISTER
The land is alive with hymns
to Apollo the Healer,
and descants of lamentation
in modes of woe.

THIRD CHORISTER
From these many afflictions,
goddess Athena,
daughter of Zeus, grant us
protection and healing.

CHORUS
Gods, goddesses, hear our fervent prayers.

FIRST CHORISTER
Ares, the savage god,
without his shield,
sends down the fire of fever,
shouting attack.

SECOND CHORISTER
Let him turn his back
and leave our land
for the Ocean of Amphitrite
or the Thracian sea.

THIRD CHORISTER
Whatever Night has spared,
Day dashes down.

Strike war god, Zeus,
with your bolts from above.

CHORUS
For you wield the power to save as well as destroy.

FIRST CHORISTER
Lord of the bright hills,
mighty Apollo,
I praise the invincible arrows
you send bringing aid.

SECOND CHORISTER
And Artemis' fiery torches
she brandishes there
in the Lycian mountains,
are signals of help.

[OEDIPUS enters from the palace.]

CHORUS
And ruddy Bacchus, too, with the turban of gold,
the Maenads' companion, to whom they cry in the night
Evohé, evohé!, draw near with torches of pinewood,
come in joy to fend off the hostile god!

Scene I

OEDIPUS
You want the plague to end and look to me.
I offer relief from our troubles, but need your help
and therefore I speak these words. Having arrived
after the deed was done, I was a stranger

and had no part in the story. A citizen now,
I nevertheless need your help in this matter,
and I issue this proclamation to all children
of Cadmus. Whoever among you knows by whose
hands Laius, Labdacus' son, was killed,
I command him to speak at once and tell me all.
Even if he himself was the culprit and fears
the penalty of death, I promise him safety.
He shall be allowed to leave our land unharmed.
But if someone who was not himself involved
has information about another—Theban
or foreigner—whom he knows to be guilty, let him
not be silent, for I can show gratitude
and dispense the rich reward that shall be his.

       Let me be clear. One who ignores this order
and keeps silent in fear for himself or a friend
should know what will happen, for I forbid all those
over whom I rule to receive him in their homes,
or speak to him, or let him share in their prayers
and sacrifices to gods, or let him touch
holy water, but all must drive him forth
because he is the source of this pollution
and the Pythia has revealed to me Apollo's
will. In the god's service do I fight
and also on behalf of the man who died.

       As for the killer, whoever he is, whether
he acted alone or with others, I pray that he suffer
a life of pain as miserable as he is.
And whoever has knowingly given him shelter, myself
included, may he suffer under this curse.

       I charge you in this for my sake, for the gods,
and for the wretched land the gods have stricken,

for even had the gods not sent this plague,
it would have been wrong to have left the land so stained
with guilt unpurified. A king was murdered.
A great man was killed, and you never found
whoever did this thing. I now hold the power
he once held, and have taken to wife the woman
he married. Had he been blessed with children, his
and mine would have had the one mother in common.
But he was childless, and therefore it is my duty
to fight on his behalf as if he had been
my own father. I shall go to any length
and do whatever is needed to hunt down
the killer of Laius, son of Labdacus, son
of Polydorus, who sprang from the ancient line
of Cadmus and before him ancient Agenor.

       For those who stand by and do nothing, I pray that the gods
may punish them as they deserve—no crops
from the earth, no children from their wives, nothing
but what afflicts us now, or even worse,
so that they perish. But to you, who approve these words
and join with me to fight for Justice, my blessings.
May the gods keep and protect you in their grace.

FIRST CHORISTER
You have put me on my oath, my Lord, and I swear
that I did not kill him or know who did. And yet
I wonder, if Apollo has sent this message,
should he not also tell us who did the crime?

OEDIPUS
That would, of course, be convenient. But one cannot force
the gods—unless they choose—to do as we'd like.

SECOND CHORISTER
May I perhaps suggest the next best thing?

OEDIPUS
Next best, or even third best. Say what it is!

SECOND CHORISTER
I am thinking of the mortal whose sight is closest
to that of Apollo. We must ask him the question.
From the great Tiresias we may learn the truth.

OEDIPUS
I have thought of that already and at Creon's
suggestion have sent two men to fetch him here.
I wonder that he has not already arrived.

FIRST CHORISTER
Everything else is rumor and speculation.

OEDIPUS
What rumors? I want to know anything that could help.

FIRST CHORISTER
It was said that he was killed by men on the road.

OEDIPUS
I've heard that, too. The question is, by whom.

FIRST CHORISTER
Whoever he is, if he has any fear within him,
having heard of your curses, he will not tarry here.

OEDIPUS
Fearless enough to commit the crime, he may not
worry too much about mere words, even mine.

SECOND CHORISTER
But here is the man who can find him and convict him,
the godlike prophet able to see the truth.

[Enter TIRESIAS, led by the BOY who guides him.]

OEDIPUS
You who know all things that can be explained
and much beyond explanation in heaven and earth,
even though you cannot see, you see
the sickness that afflicts the city and even
the reason for that sickness. Tiresias, you
are the champion we need, the protector and guide.
No doubt you have heard the word that comes from Delphi.
The god has told us the end of the plague would come
only if we found the killers of Laius
and either killed them or sent them into exile.
Do then whatever you do, with birds or other
means of divination to save yourself,
the city, me, and all of us from pollution
that attaches to that death. We are in your hands.
For you to use your gifts in such a crisis
and help us with your insight would be most noble.

TIRESIAS
How terrible it is to have the knowledge
that does the one who knows it no good at all.
I know, but know enough to have kept quiet.
I would not, on my own, have come here today.

OEDIPUS
What's wrong? Why do you seem so spiritless?

TIRESIAS
Let me go home again. Do as I say.
It will be better that way for both of us.

OEDIPUS
That is unhelpful and unfriendly. To this
great city that reared you, you owe more than silence.

TIRESIAS
Your speech misses the mark, and I fear that the same
would happen to me if I were to speak.

OEDIPUS
                              If you know,
I beg you, tell us. Do not turn away. I implore you,
as do all of us here.

TIRESIAS
                    You are ignorant, all.
I shall never reveal my sorrows. Or speak of yours.

OEDIPUS
What are you telling us? You know but refuse
to help? That you will betray and destroy the city?

TIRESIAS
I do not want to give pain to you or myself.
You question me in vain. You will learn nothing.

OEDIPUS
Most wicked of wicked men, you would enrage
a rock! What kind of prophet knows but will not
say, silent, proud, and utterly useless?

TIRESIAS
You blame my anger, but you do not see your own.
Only look at yourself, finding fault with me.

OEDIPUS
Who would not be angry, hearing your words
and seeing the lack of respect you show the city?

TIRESIAS
Even if I keep silent, the evil will out.

OEDIPUS
Is that not a reason for you to tell me now?

TIRESIAS
I will say not another word. Now, rage
as much as you like at me and vent your anger.

OEDIPUS
I am infuriated enough to say
what I begin to suspect—that you yourself
took some part in the killing, inciting, or planning.
You did not, with your own hands, commit the murder,
but if you were not blind, I wouldn't have ruled that out.

TIRESIAS
[after a pause]
Very well, then. I call on you to obey
that proclamation of yours, and do not speak
to me or to anyone here. For you are the one.
Unholy, you are the one who pollutes of this land.

OEDIPUS
Wild and shameless. You think you can get away
with making such an implausible accusation?

TIRESIAS
I have escaped already. The truth protects me.

OEDIPUS
From whom did you get this? Or did you dream this up
by your prophetic art?

TIRESIAS
                    I got it from you.
You were the one who forced me to speak up.

OEDIPUS
I forced you? Then say it again more clearly.
Tell me so that I understand what you mean.

TIRESIAS
What I said was perfectly clear, I think.

OEDIPUS
Clear to you but to nobody else. Explain it.

TIRESIAS
You are the murderer you are looking for.

OEDIPUS
You have the gall to repeat this outrageous charge?

TIRESIAS
Would you like to hear something to make you angrier still?

OEDIPUS
Go ahead, as long as you're wasting breath.

TIRESIAS
I tell you then that, although you are unaware,
you and your loved ones are living in shameful
relationships that men would call loathsome.

OEDIPUS
You dare to say such things? You even enjoy it!

TIRESIAS
What I dare is simply to love the truth.

OEDIPUS
What would you know of truth? You are blind not only
in eyes but in ears and also in your mind.

TIRESIAS
Go on, insult me. The time will come soon enough
when you shall be hearing worse, everywhere always.

OEDIPUS
In the constant darkness in which you live, you cannot
hurt me or anyone else who sees in the light.

TIRESIAS
Your fall will not be of my doing. Apollo
has it in mind himself to bring this about.

OEDIPUS
Did Creon say this? Or is this your idea?

TIRESIAS
Never mind Creon. The trouble is in yourself.

OEDIPUS
In a way, I agree with you—that riches and talent
and kingly power provoke envy and hatred.
What the city placed in my hands as a free-will gift
I never asked for. The power to rule has resulted
in Creon's transparent machinations. My friend,
my wife's brother, has set upon me with plots
and longs to supplant me. He sets upon me this wizard,
this scheming beggar, blind except for the vision
of profit that shines bright before him. His art
of seeing into the past and future is merely
greed. Remember the Sphinx with her terrible riddle?
If you were such a seer, why could you not
answer her question and save the citizens? What
did your claims about signs from birds and hints from gods
add up to? I was the one who hit the mark,
using my native wits, without any foolish
flights of birds overhead. You still resent it
and hope to stand close by Creon's side
when he sits on the throne and to whisper into his ear.
Ambition, greed, and envy! But you and he
will regret this treacherous venture. You want to exploit
the plague and my curse as a way to get rid of me.
Were you not old and blind and feeble, you'd know
how dangerous are such vile thoughts and actions.

FIRST CHORISTER
It appears to us that both of you have spoken
in anger, which is seldom helpful. We need
to consider how to respond to the oracle's words.

TIRESIAS
You are the king, but even so, we must be
equals in answering harsh words for harsh words.
I am not your slave but that of the god Apollo,
and I am not Creon's partisan or henchman.
You have reproached me with blindness, but I say
that although you may have sight, you cannot see
what trouble you are in, or even with whom
you share your home. Do you know who your parents were?
Have you any idea that you are an enemy
to them, both living and dead? The curse that comes
from your mother and father approaches with deadly steps
and one day it shall drive you out of this land.
You can see now, but do not. Soon, a blind man,
you will one day see nothing at all but darkness.
The mountainsides of Helicon and Cithaeron
shall echo your wails of woe when you understand
your marriage and what a dangerous harbor it was
into which you sailed on what you thought was a fair
wind. Other troubles shall come that you cannot
imagine to you and your children, too. Go ahead,
berate Creon, insult my prophetic words,
but there is no one among all mortals who shall be
more shunned and cruelly used than you.

OEDIPUS
This is beyond endurance. Can I bear
to hear such words from such a man? Go,
get out of here, away from me and this house.

TIRESIAS
I would never have come, had I not been sent for.

OEDIPUS
I did not expect such drivel. Had I known,
I never would have summoned you here to the palace.

TIRESIAS
You think I am foolish? The parents who gave you birth
considered me wise enough and listened to me.

OEDIPUS
What parents? Wait! Who were they who gave me birth?

TIRESIAS
Today shall be your parent and your gravedigger.

OEDIPUS
You speak in riddles.

TIRESIAS
                              You are good at riddles.

OEDIPUS
You insult my great achievement?

TIRESIAS
                              You'll see what it got you.

OEDIPUS
My answer saved the city. That's what matters.

TIRESIAS
Fine. I will go now. Boy, take me away.

OEDIPUS
Yes, let him take you away. Here, you're a nuisance,
and when you are gone we'll all be better off.

TIRESIAS
I'm going. You and I have spoken of grave
matters that brought me here. I am not afraid,
for you can do nothing to hurt me. And I say this:
that man you are looking for, with your threats and edicts
about the killer of Laius . . . That man is here.
It is said that he is a stranger who came to Thebes,
but it will turn out that he is a native Theban,
although this will not be welcome news to him.
He shall wander over strange lands, a blind man
who once had sight, a poor man who once
had wealth, feeling his way along the road
with a stick. And he shall discover that he is,
to his children, not only father but also brother,
and to his mother both a son and husband.
And to his father, the sharer of his wife,
and the murderer!
                    Now go and consider this,
and if I have been wrong in any detail,
you may say I have no skill in prophecy.

[TIRESIAS exits, led by the BOY. OEDIPUS exits into the palace.]

Ode I

FIRST CHORISTER
Who is this man the oracle means?
Who did that unspeakable thing and bloodied his hands?
Now is the time for him to run
on quick feet, faster than fastest
horses, for after him comes the son of Zeus

with lightning's deadly fire and, close on his heels,
the Spirits of Death that never miss their mark.

SECOND CHORISTER
From the snowy heights of Parnassus, the voice
sang out to order Thebans to hunt down
this unknown culprit, a beast that lurks
in savage jungles, hides in caves,
and scampers over the rocks, or a bull with a wounded
foot that hirples along, fleeing words
that well from earth to hover about his head.

FIRST CHORISTER
Terrible, terrible trouble Tiresias brings.
I do not believe it; I do not disbelieve it.
I have no idea what to say.
I soar on wings of hope but fear the height.
I cannot read the future; I cannot read
the present, either.
What were Labdacus' quarrels?
What were the grudges of Polybus, King of Corinth?
I never knew and never wanted to know.
But what am I to think of Oedipus now?
Do we dare oppose him, seeking justice
for Laius' murder?

SECOND CHORISTER
Apollo is wise, and Zeus truly is wise.
Looking down, they know the affairs of men.
But mortals here on earth,
how can we tell if a prophet is wiser than we are?
There are different kinds of wisdom one may use
for differing ends.

But Oedipus? How can I doubt him?
I saw with my own eyes the wingèd Sphinx
assail him, and he withstood her and by his wits
bested her and saved us. I cannot now,
knowing how dear he is to the city,
think him guilty.

Scene II

[Enter CREON, from stage left.]

CREON
Citizens, I am here to defend myself
against the outrageous accusations I hear
that Oedipus has made against me. They're wrong!
Utterly groundless. If I had done him harm
in any way, either by word or deed,
I'd be ashamed and should not want to live!
This is a grave matter. He calls me a traitor
to the city and to each of you, my friends.

FIRST CHORISTER
That is, indeed, what he said, but perhaps he spoke
in anger and in the heat of a bad moment.

CREON
But he said that the prophet lied. And he said that I
was the one who had persuaded or bribed him to do so!

SECOND CHORISTER
That is what he said. But he couldn't have meant it.

CREON
Was he rolling his eyes or looking straight ahead?
Did he seem to any of you like a man gone mad?

FIRST CHORISTER
How are we to judge the minds of our rulers?

SECOND CHORISTER
But here he comes. You can answer your question yourself.

[Enter OEDIPUS.]

OEDIPUS

[To CREON.]
You dare to show your face? You come to my house,
a man who killed the king and now wants me dead.
You want to take the throne? You have some nerve!
But answer me: why you have undertaken
this treason? Did you see some fault in me?
Some sign of folly or weakness? Did you think
I would not be able to recognize a plot,
however stealthy, when it attacked me? Did you
suppose I could not act to defend myself?
What made you think that you could succeed without
money, without friends, without support?

CREON
Do you know what you should do? Listen, as I
have listened to you. Then you can make your judgment.

OEDIPUS
You are a clever speaker, but I am not good
at listening to the words of a friend who has turned
foe.

CREON
      Well, first of all, listen to this.

OEDIPUS
Well, first of all, admit that you are a traitor.

CREON
Stubbornness without wisdom will do you no
good. You are not thinking clearly.

OEDIPUS
                  And harm
to a kinsman is your idea of wisdom? Or prudence?

CREON
That's perfectly true. But what are you saying I did?

OEDIPUS
You were the one who told me to send for the prophet!

CREON
Yes, I was. And I stand by that advice.

OEDIPUS
[after a pause]
How long ago did Laius . . . ?

CREON
                  Did Laius what?

OEDIPUS
Disappear. Get killed. How long ago?

CREON
Many years ago. A long time.

OEDIPUS
And this prophet? He was here, then, prophesying?

CREON
Yes, and honored as much as he is now.

OEDIPUS
Back then, did he make any mention of me?

CREON
                                        No,
I don't think so. Certainly not to me.

OEDIPUS
And you made no attempt to find the killer?

CREON
We did. But we got absolutely nowhere.

OEDIPUS
And why did this wise man say nothing then?

CREON
I can't answer. I haven't the least idea.

OEDIPUS
But it's staring you in the face. How can you miss it?

CREON
What's staring me in the face? What do you mean?

OEDIPUS
There's no other reason for him to accuse me now
of killing Laius except that you and he
are plotting together.

CREON
He couldn't have said that! I've answered your
questions, and claim the right to ask my own.

OEDIPUS
Whatever questions you like. I'm not the killer.

CREON
You are married to my sister, are you not?

OEDIPUS
Yes, of course. As everyone knows.

CREON
                                                        And you
and she share the rule of the land.

OEDIPUS
                                                Yes,
as equals. She has whatever power she wants.

CREON
And I, too, am an equal in this arrangement?

OEDIPUS
Yes, and that's exactly what makes you a traitor.

CREON

Not if you look at the question objectively.
Ask yourself why I would want to rule
in fear when I have all I want this way
and am able to sleep soundly. Why would a man
who has all the power he wants be greedy for more?
The only thing I don't have is the headaches
that come with being the ruler. It makes no sense!
If I were king, I'd have to do all manner
of disagreeable things. I'm not a fool
and know when I have enough to satisfy me.
People greet me, salute me, curry favor,
and treat me with all deference. What more could I ask?

You doubt me? Go to the oracle at Delphi
and ask what the Pytho said. I reported it truly
and accurately. Then look into this business
of whether the prophet and I conspired together,
and if you find any shred of evidence, judge me
and condemn me to death, not just with your own vote
but mine as well. But don't just dream up guesses
and suppose they must be true. That is unjust
and altogether wrong—to think good men
bad and bad men good. In the course of time
you'll see—for in all human affairs time
brings the truth to light. Only time will show you
who is the loyal kinsman, but the traitor
is likely to be revealed in a single day.

FIRST CHORISTER

He has spoken well. To a careful man like me,
it's right to be thorough and safer to take one's time.

OEDIPUS
If the conspiracy moves quickly, it makes no sense
for me to drag my feet. That way, I'd lose.

CREON
What do you want? To exile me from Thebes?

OEDIPUS
Banishment isn't enough. I want your death.

CREON
Excessive, is it not? It makes you look spiteful.

OEDIPUS
{Why on earth should I listen to your advice?}[1]

CREON
You don't seem willing to take *any* advice!

OEDIPUS
{You think that I am entirely out of my mind?}

CREON
Yes, and you are also a faithless friend.

OEDIPUS
I am faithful to myself.

CREON
                                    But not to me.

OEDIPUS
But you are a traitor.

CREON

And you, sir, are a fool!

OEDIPUS
Still, I have to rule.

CREON

But you're doing it badly.

OEDIPUS
I think of the city. The city!

CREON

So do I,
for I have a share in the city as well as you.

SECOND CHORISTER
My lords, get hold of yourselves. Jocasta is coming.
Perhaps with her help you can settle this dreadful quarrel.

[JOCASTA enters from the palace.]

JOCASTA
Deplorable! For two grown men to quarrel,
insulting each other when the city is so sick
and requires some more intelligent response!
This is neither the time nor place. Oedipus,
go inside. And you, Creon, go home.
and stop pestering us with your petty complaints.

CREON
Sister, this is important. Oedipus threatens
truly dreadful things—either to kill me
or else drive me from Thebes and into exile.

OEDIPUS
What he says is correct—I have discovered
his scheme to do me terrible bodily harm.

CREON
I take a solemn oath, may gods strike me
dead if I have done what you say I have.

JOCASTA
Oedipus, why don't you believe him? He swears
a solemn oath before the gods, and me,
and all these men, to which you should give respect.

FIRST CHORISTER
My lord, I beg you, listen to what she says.

OEDIPUS
What is it that you want me to agree to?

FIRST CHORISTER
Creon's reputation for telling the truth
in the past, and now the solemn oath he has taken.

OEDIPUS
But do you know what you want me to do?

FIRST CHORISTER
                                                    Yes.

OEDIPUS
Then tell me. Spell it out. What are you proposing?

FIRST CHORISTER
That you should not make these speculative charges
against your friend who has taken his holy oath.

OEDIPUS
You understand that what you ask implies
my own death or at least my exile.

FIRST CHORISTER
                                        No,
I swear by the Sun, the foremost of all the gods!
May I perish at once, may my friends shun me, may all
the gods turn away, if I had any such thought.
The sorry state in which we find our land
breaks my heart, and this new trouble adds
new weight to those that already press us down.

OEDIPUS
Let him go, then, even if it means
that I must die, or in dishonor be driven
out into exile? Your words have aroused
pity in me—however much I hate him.

CREON
You can't even yield with grace, but your ill will
poisons whatever you do. How in the world
can you stand yourself?

OEDIPUS
                                Just leave me alone. Go.

CREON
Gladly. With you I got nowhere. They saved me.

[Exit CREON to stage right.]

FIRST CHORISTER
Madam, you ought to take him inside now.

JOCASTA
I will, as soon as I've learned what's going on.

FIRST CHORISTER
Extravagant accusations were made. But even
a baseless charge carries a certain sting.

JOCASTA
They came from both sides?

FIRST CHORISTER
                                        Yes.

JOCASTA
                              What did they say?

FIRST CHORISTER
Enough, enough! Better to let it lie.
Better for us and for the country's sake.

OEDIPUS
You see where this is going? I search for the truth
and you are not helping me or my enterprise.

FIRST CHORISTER
My lord, I am always loyal to you. And grateful.
When we were in that sea of troubles before,
you were the one who found a fair wind and steered us
to safety, as I trust you will do again.

JOCASTA
I entreat you, my lord, tell me why you are angry.

OEDIPUS
I will, madam, for your opinion counts
more with me than that of all these people.
Creon has been plotting to overthrow me.

JOCASTA
Tell me what you mean. What has he done?

OEDIPUS
He accuses me of being Laius' killer.

JOCASTA
From his own knowledge? Or did he hear this from someone?

OEDIPUS
He sent that villainous prophet to make the charge.
That way he didn't have to say it himself.

JOCASTA
Then pay it no mind. Who believes in prophets?
No mortal can see into the future. I
can prove this to you. An oracle came to Laius
from one of Apollo's servants once to warn him
that he was fated to die at the hands of a son
born to him and me. But as we know,
Laius was killed by robbers at that crossroads
where three roads come together. And it couldn't have been
the child we had. When he was three days old,
Laius had his ankles pierced and bound
together and set him out on the mountain to perish
so Apollo could not work his dreadful will.
He couldn't have lived to kill his father, and Laius
couldn't have died at the hands of his own son.

The oracle was perfectly clear—but wrong.
So never mind about it. What the gods do,
they do, and we learn their will directly from them.

OEDIPUS
What? My mind wandered there for a moment,
and I had an uneasy feeling.

JOCASTA
Do you know what it was?

OEDIPUS
I thought I heard you say that Laius was murdered
at a place where three roads meet . . .

JOCASTA
                                        That was the story.

OEDIPUS
And where is the place this thing was said to have happened?

JOCASTA
In Phocis, where the road diverges. One goes
to Delphi and the other off toward Daulis.

OEDIPUS
And how long ago was it that this thing happened?

JOCASTA
It was just before you arrived and became king.

OEDIPUS
O Zeus! How have you plotted against me?

JOCASTA
Oedipus, what is it? What's the matter?

OEDIPUS
Don't ask me yet. Tell me about Laius.
How old was he? Did he look young? Describe him.

JOCASTA
He was dark but his hair had started to show some white
at the temples. He looked . . . a little bit like you.

OEDIPUS
Omoi! That curse! I may have cursed myself.

JOCASTA
What is it, my lord? That awful look on your face . . .

OEDIPUS
I have a terrible feeling that the blind prophet
may not have been so blind. Tell me one thing.

JOCASTA
Yes, whatever you want to know. But I'm frightened.

OEDIPUS
How many guards did he have? A few? Many?

JOCASTA
Five, I think. One of them was a herald.
There was only a single carriage for the king.

OEDIPUS
Aieee! It all comes clear. Who told you this?

JOCASTA
A slave, the only one to come back alive.

OEDIPUS
Is he still here as part of the household?

JOCASTA
No. When he returned and saw that you
were the king, he took my hand as a suppliant
and begged me to send him out into the fields,
as far away from the city as he could be.
I thought he deserved it and granted him that favor.

OEDIPUS
Could he come back here right away?

JOCASTA
                                    Of course.
But what do you want him for? What can he tell you?

OEDIPUS
I have said too much already. I need to see him.

JOCASTA
Then he shall come. But may I not know why?

OEDIPUS
You deserve to. Who in the world has a better
right to hear the story and know what I'm going
through as we approach the crisis.
                                    My father
was Polybus of Corinth, and my mother
was a Dorian, Merope. I lived in the palace
where I grew up among the leaders of the city

in greatest comfort which I had done nothing to earn
and took more or less for granted. At dinner one night
a man got drunk and in his cups he said
I was not my father's child. I was furious then
and could barely control myself. The next day I asked
my mother and father if this had just been an empty
insult or if he knew something I didn't.
They made the drunk pay dearly for what he'd done,
and for a while I was content, but still
I kept thinking about it. Eventually,
without my parents' knowledge, I went to Delphi
to ask Apollo's oracle for the truth.
She didn't give me an answer but told me horrid,
dreadful things that I hated to hear, saying
that I would lie with my mother and bring forth children
the world would hate to look at, and that I would be
the murderer of the father who sired me.

      When I learned this, I left Corinth at once,
making out my position by the stars
and getting as far away as I could to prevent
such terrible predictions from coming true.
I was making my way when I came to the place you describe,
where the king met his end. And I shudder to say it, but there
three roads met. This is the awful truth.
And there was a man in a carriage, and there was a herald,
just as you've described it. The driver tried
and the old man himself rudely attempted
to force me from the road, but in my anger
I struck him, that driver who had blocked my way.
The old man in the carriage bided his time
and, when I passed, he hit the side of my head
with his pointed goad. And I paid him back with a stick

[handwritten marginal notes: The past systematically brought back in this play — the shepherd, the messenger]

I had in my hand. I struck him with it hard,
and he rolled out of the carriage, and I killed him
and all the others, too. If that man had
any connection at all with Laius, then I
am the saddest, the most miserable of men.
Who could be more detestable to the gods
than I, whom no one, citizen or stranger,
can address, or have in his home—for I myself
laid this terrible curse upon myself.

   If that was Laius, I am polluting the bed
of a dead man with the hands that took his life.
Am I the criminal? Am I not obscene
and altogether unholy? Must I leave
my country and never see my loved ones again?
I cannot go back to Corinth, lest I risk
marriage with my mother and shedding the blood
of Polybus who begot me and brought me up.
Some cruel god is at work! I cannot bear it!
Never may I see that terrible day the mighty
gods seem to have contemplated for me,
but let me wholly vanish from among men
before my life is stained by such a disaster.

FIRST CHORISTER
This is dreadful, my lord, but do not give up
all hope until we hear from the man who was there.

OEDIPUS
There is one detail I hope to hear from the herdsman.

JOCASTA
When he arrives, what is it that you hope for?

OEDIPUS

One vital thing you said that he may confirm.

JOCASTA

And what was that?

OEDIPUS

                        You said that he said "robbers."
If he still uses the plural, then I am saved
and could not have been the killer. One and many
are not the same, after all. But if he says
it was a single man, then the balance shifts.

JOCASTA

"Robbers" was what he said at the time, and now
he cannot change his story. The entire city
heard him, not just me. In any case,
he can never prove that Laius' murder was what
Apollo foretold—to die at the hands of my son.
That poor child never killed anyone,
but perished years before on that mountainside.
So what do prophecies mean? Nothing at all!

OEDIPUS

I am somewhat reassured. Still, send for the slave.

JOCASTA

I shall do so at once, my lord. Whatever you want.
Meanwhile, let us go, you and I, inside.

Ode II

FIRST CHORISTER
I pray for a fate that allows me
praise for my words and deeds
as models of strict observance
of heaven's laws
handed down from Olympus.
They are not merely mortal
and never expire or lapse
but, like the gods who gave them,
continue in power forever.

SECOND CHORISTER
Hubris will beget
a tyrant as its child,
where insolence and greed
mount to the pediment
or rush to the lip of the chasm
where feet can find no purchase.
But decent competition
brings profit to the city,
and the gods approve and protect it.

FIRST CHORISTER
If an insolent man ignores
Justice and fails to revere
the gods, a terrible fate
will overwhelm him and punish
his overweening pride and his taking advantage
and desecrating what's holy.
He shall dance in a shower of arrows
he cannot avoid or evade.

Why, otherwise, would we pray
to the gods and dance our dances?

SECOND CHORISTER
If the oracles do not speak truly,
why should we go to Delphi,
the temple at Abae in Phocis,
or Olympia for unreliable words?
But you, Zeus, who are called
lord of the world, hark,
for the oracles' power is fading,
and the words about Laius expunged.
Apollo is disesteemed
and the power of gods is ending.

Scene III

[Enter JOCASTA, carrying offerings of flowers for one of the altars.]

JOCASTA

[To the CHORUS.]
Lords of the land, the thought occurred to me
that bearing these garlands I should appeal to the gods.
Oedipus' mind is in turmoil, his grief is beyond him,
and he seizes upon whatever the latest person
has said, whether good or bad.
[Turning to speak to the heavens.]
                              His balance is gone.
I can do no good talking to him, so I turn
to you, Apollo, who are, as it were, our neighbor
in nearby Delphi. I pray that you may supply us

with help, some purification, some solution
to these insoluble problems. We see him, our captain,
powerless now, and we are all afraid.

[Enter MESSENGER.]

MESSENGER
Strangers, I am a stranger here, and I ask
where is King Oedipus' house, or better,
if you can tell me, where is the man himself.

FIRST CHORISTER
This is his dwelling, behind us. He is at home.
And this is his wife and mother of his children.

MESSENGER
May she then, being his consort, and all of you
be ever happy with the news I bring.

JOCASTA
And may you be happy as well, as you deserve
for your courtesy. Now, tell us, what is your news?

MESSENGER
Good news indeed for him and his house.

JOCASTA
                                    Tell us.
And tell us also where it is that you come from.

MESSENGER
From Corinth, and the word I speak is good,
but not without its element of sorrow.

JOCASTA
What are you saying? What is its double power?

MESSENGER
The Corinthians want to have Oedipus as their king.

JOCASTA
What? Is the old King Polybus not still in power?

MESSENGER
No, alas. He has died and is in his tomb.

JOCASTA
Oedipus' father is dead? Is that what you're saying?

MESSENGER
I hope to die if I am not telling the truth.

JOCASTA

[To a SERVANT.]
Go at once and tell this to your master.

[SERVANT exits into the palace.]
O gods, where are you now with your prophecies
and dire warnings? Oedipus kept this man
at a distance for fear of killing him some day,
and now the man has died, and not at his hand!

[Enter OEDIPUS.]

OEDIPUS
Dearest wife, why have you summoned me here?

JOCASTA
Listen to what this messenger has to tell you
and then stop fretting about the gods and fate.

OEDIPUS
Who is he? What is he going to say?

JOCASTA
                                    He comes
from Corinth to bring you the news that your father is dead.

OEDIPUS
What? Is this true, stranger? Tell me yourself!

MESSENGER
Yes, what she says is true. He is dead and gone.

OEDIPUS
Was it treason or crime, or was it from natural causes?

MESSENGER
For the old, even a little bump will do.

OEDIPUS
He fell ill and died, then. I'm sad to hear it.

MESSENGER
Illness, or perhaps it was sheer old age.

OEDIPUS
Oh, me! Oh, me! The Pythia speaks and we listen,
and the birds crisscross the skies overhead and we look,
but what do they mean? What have they got to tell us?
I was supposed to kill my father, she said,

but he is dead and I am here, far away,
and have not touched a weapon. Unless he died
from missing me, which is not very likely, I
had nothing at all to do with it. Nothing whatever.
Polybus lies in Hades shades, and with him
all those dreadful oracles' hollow words
worth nothing now or ever.

JOCASTA

Did I not say so?

OEDIPUS
You did, but I was afraid and did not believe you.

JOCASTA
Now you can, and your worries at last are ended.

OEDIPUS
And I don't have to fear that I'll have sex with my mother!

JOCASTA
There is no way to know the future. What we do
we do on our own: there's no sense being afraid
of what may be fated. We live however we can,
making our choices day by day. You do not
need to worry further about your mother.
It is only in dreams that men find themselves in their mothers'
beds. But this is a waking world, and men
live better who do not fret about such things.

OEDIPUS
That's all reassuring. I almost believe you.
But still my mother lives, and I am afraid.

JOCASTA
Your father's funeral ought to give you courage.

OEDIPUS
It does, but as long as she lives, I have to be worried.

MESSENGER
Who is this woman that makes you live in fear?

OEDIPUS
Merope, my mother. Polybus' widow.

MESSENGER
What is it, sir, that causes you to fear her?

OEDIPUS
A prophecy from the oracle, old fellow.

MESSENGER
Can you tell me what it was the oracle said?

OEDIPUS
Absolutely. Apollo said I would lie
with my mother and shed my father's blood with my own
hands. That is the reason I've stayed away
from Corinth. I've done well, as you see, but a man
misses his home and the faces of his parents.

MESSENGER
It was fear of them that made you leave?

OEDIPUS
                                        Yes,
for who likes the idea of killing his father?

MESSENGER
I come in friendship and would be glad to release you
from the fear you have been living with so long.

OEDIPUS
And you shall receive an appropriate reward.

MESSENGER
That is what I'd hoped for—that when you return
home to Corinth, you would do well for me.

OEDIPUS
I cannot go back there while a parent lives.

MESSENGER
My son, it seems you don't know what you are doing.

OEDIPUS
What do you mean, old man? Explain yourself.

MESSENGER
It was because of them that you stayed away?

OEDIPUS
Yes, as I've said. I feared Apollo's words.

MESSENGER
You're worried about your parents? Is that what it is?

OEDIPUS
Yes, yes! Exactly.

MESSENGER
                    Then you have no reason to fear!

OEDIPUS
But these are my parents. How can I not worry?

MESSENGER
Polybus is not related to you.

OEDIPUS
What? He was my father!

MESSENGER
                              No more than I was.
Or just as much.

OEDIPUS
                    What are you talking about?
You're nothing to me.

MESSENGER
                         Well, I did not beget you.
But neither did he.

OEDIPUS
                    He always called me his son!

MESSENGER
Let me explain. I brought you to him. A gift.

OEDIPUS
I wasn't his son? And even so, he loved me? *Human relationship*
Why was that?   *— that has some pathos*
                                             This was his childhood
MESSENGER
                    He had no child of his own.

Just as Jocasta
gave up her infant

OEDIPUS
Where did you get me? Did you find me? Buy me?

MESSENGER
I found you on the side of Mount Cithaeron.

OEDIPUS
And what were you doing there?

MESSENGER
                                Grazing my flock
on the lower slopes of the mountain. I was a shepherd.

OEDIPUS
A shepherd, just out there looking after your flock?

MESSENGER
Yes, and I found you there, my son—as it were.

OEDIPUS
When you found me, was I suffering at all?

MESSENGER
Your ankles would still trouble you.

OEDIPUS
                                And why
do you mention my injury of so long ago?

MESSENGER
Your tendons had been pierced and bound together.

OEDIPUS
It has been a source of shame, even from the cradle.

MESSENGER
That was how you got your name—Swell-Foot.

OEDIPUS
Good gods! Did my father or mother give me that name?

MESSENGER
I've no idea. Ask him who gave you to me.

OEDIPUS
Then you didn't find me. You got me from someone else?

MESSENGER
Yes, from another shepherd there on the mountain.

OEDIPUS
Who was he? Do you remember his name?

MESSENGER
                                        No,
but I know that he was one of Laius' men.

OEDIPUS
Laius, the man who ruled in Thebes?

MESSENGER
                                        Yes,
the shepherd was part of his household. I'm sure of that.

OEDIPUS
And is he still alive? Can I speak to him?

MESSENGER
I've no idea. I'm a stranger. Your people would know.

OEDIPUS

[To the CHORUS.]
Does anybody here know that shepherd?
Is he here in Thebes or somewhere out in the fields?
It is time that we get some answers to these questions.

FIRST CHORISTER
I think he is the same man that you wanted
a while ago and sent for. But Jocasta
could probably tell you better than any of us.

OEDIPUS
Lady, is this fellow we sent for the same?

JOCASTA
Never mind. Just . . . let it go. Forget it.

OEDIPUS
Having heard this much? How can I not go ahead
and find out the truth of my birth and who I am?

JOCASTA
I beg you. Drop it! If you care at all
for me, or for yourself and your life. Stop this!

OEDIPUS
What do you have to worry about? I promise,
even if I turn out to have been born
from third-generation slaves, you will not be
affected by this, or damaged or demeaned.

JOCASTA
I beg you. I implore you. Do not do this.

OEDIPUS
You'll never persuade me to give up my search for the truth.

JOCASTA
To hell with the truth. I'm saying what's best for you.

OEDIPUS
That "best" has caused me torment all my life.

JOCASTA
You have no idea who you are. May you never find out!

OEDIPUS
Will someone bring that god-damned shepherd here?
Let her go worry about her noble blood.

JOCASTA
Unfortunate man! You poor unhappy fool!
There is nothing more I can say to you. Ever.

[Exit JOCASTA into the palace.]

FIRST CHORISTER
What could be wrong? She seems to be in pain.
She says nothing, but I am afraid that when
she breaks her silence, evil will pour forth.

OEDIPUS
Let it come, whatever it is. I want
to learn who I am and where I came from. Proud
as women often are, she's ashamed of my birth,
but my life has brought good to me and to Thebes as well
and it shall not be dishonored. I am Fortune's
child, and the months that have brought me from small to great

are my brothers and sisters. With such a mother as Fortune
has been to me, how can I stop now
and not discover the details of my birth?

[OEDIPUS remains on stage during the Third Ode.]

Ode III

FIRST CHORISTER
If anyone can learn anything, know
anything, then, O Cithaeron,
tomorrow's full moon shall crown you,
as mother and nurse of Oedipus. We do you
honor in our dances for succoring princes.
And to you, great Apollo, we raise our voices
and ask that you may accept our prayers.

SECOND CHORISTER
We wonder who, among the immortals, bore you?
And who was your father? Was it Pan,
who roves the wooded glens and hillsides?
Or was your mother's bedfellow Apollo,
who loves the wild woodlands? Or Hermes,
Lord of Cyllene, or Dionysos to whom
one of Helicon's dark-eyed nymphs gave you?

Scene IV

OEDIPUS
I think that may be the shepherd we're waiting for.
I've never seen him before, but he's the right age.

And those people with him, I'm sure they are my servants.
But you know who he is. Am I guessing right?

FIRST CHORISTER
Yes, you are quite correct. I recognize him.
He was as faithful a servant as Laius had,
even if he was out there herding sheep.

[Enter SHEPHERD.]

OEDIPUS
You, sir, from Corinth. Is this the man you mean?

MESSENGER
That's him.

OEDIPUS
                              You there, old man! Look at me,
and answer my questions! Did you belong to Laius?

SHEPHERD
Yes, I was a slave. Not bought but raised here.

OEDIPUS
And what work did you do? What trade did you follow?

SHEPHERD
For most of my life, I have been a herdsman.

OEDIPUS
And where did you take your herds? Where did you camp?

SHEPHERD
Mostly in the low hills near Cithaeron.

OEDIPUS
Have you met this man? Have you ever seen him before?

SHEPHERD
What man do you mean? Met him doing what?

OEDIPUS
This man! Have you ever had dealings with him?

SHEPHERD
I don't believe so. Not that I can remember.

MESSENGER
It's not surprising, after all this time.
But let me refresh his memory, my lord.
I know, and I think he will remember as well,
that both of us had our herds on Cithaeron. He
had two and I had one. And we were out there
for six months at a time, from spring to fall.
This happened three years running, and then when winter
was coming, I would drive my flocks to their pens,
and he'd take his back to Laius' sheepfolds.

[To SHEPHERD.]
Is what I am saying true? Or is it not?

SHEPHERD
It was a long time ago, but . . . yes, it's true.

MESSENGER
And do you not remember that you gave me
a baby once, to bring up as my own?

SHEPHERD
Why do you ask these questions? Leave me alone!

MESSENGER

[To the SHEPHERD.]
This is the man, my friend, who was then the child.

SHEPHERD

[Menacing the MESSENGER.]
Damn it, will you just shut your mouth?

OEDIPUS
No, old man. Don't chastise him. Your words
deserve a reprimand sooner than his.

SHEPHERD
                                        But master,
what is my offense?

OEDIPUS
                                You do not answer.
You don't say anything about that child.

SHEPHERD
He doesn't know what he's talking about. He's raving.

OEDIPUS
If kindness gets us nowhere, we can try pain.

SHEPHERD
I'm an old man. I beg you, no torture, please.

OEDIPUS
Somebody tie his hands behind his back.

SHEPHERD
Oh, woe! Why? What do you want to know?

OEDIPUS
Did you give this man the child he's asking about?

SHEPHERD
I did. And I wish I'd died on that same day.

OEDIPUS
You'll die on this one if you don't answer my questions.

SHEPHERD
If I do, my ruin is every bit as certain.

OEDIPUS
You're stalling, and my patience is wearing thin.

SHEPHERD
I'm not stalling. I told you. I gave him the child.

OEDIPUS
And from whom did you get it? Was it your own? Or whose?

SHEPHERD
It wasn't my own. I got it . . . from someone else.

OEDIPUS
From whom, then? From what person? Of what rank?

SHEPHERD
Master, I beg you. No more questions, please!

OEDIPUS
If I have to ask once more, you're a dead man.

SHEPHERD
I got it from someone in the house of Laius.

OEDIPUS
A slave or a family member?

SHEPHERD
                              Merciful gods!
I've come to the breaking point in this.

OEDIPUS
                                          And I
have come to the breaking point in hearing this!
Go on! Speak!

SHEPHERD
                    It was said to be Laius' child.
But your wife, inside, could tell you better than I.

OEDIPUS
She gave it to you.

SHEPHERD
                    Yes, my lord.

OEDIPUS
                                          Why?

SHEPHERD
So I could kill it.

OEDIPUS

Poor woman! She was its mother?

SHEPHERD

Yes. There had been prophecies.

OEDIPUS

Of what?

SHEPHERD

It was said that the child would one day kill its parents.

OEDIPUS

Then how was it that you gave the child to him?

SHEPHERD

My lord, I felt sorry for it. I thought
he'd take it far away, to another country
where he was from. He kept it alive, but it seems
only for a greater disaster—if you
are the child he says you are, you were born to grief.

OEDIPUS

Ohhhh! Ohhhh! Now it comes clear. O light!
I look on you for the last time. Cursed in my birth
and life, cursed in my marriage, and cursed in my killing.

[OEDIPUS exits into the palace. The MESSENGER and
SHEPHERD exit, right.]

Ode IV

FIRST CHORISTER
Alas! The generations of men
in their effort, honor, achievement, their pride . . .
and in the end it comes to nothing.
What man, after chasing all his life
for the shadow of happiness, can claim
more than a moment's illusion?
Oedipus, your fate
is a chilling example.
You had everything that makes for happiness,
and in a moment, it's gone.

SECOND CHORISTER
Your arrows always flew to the target
accurate and amazing. Whatever you wanted,
there it was, in an instant,
almost without effort, more than the gods
ever intended for mere mortals.
Even Zeus was startled
to see you destroy
the Sphinx, that cruel maiden with terrible talons,
protecting us all from death.

CHORUS
Because of what you did, we called you our king,
giving you all honor, and you ruled mighty Thebes.

FIRST CHORISTER
And now? Whose story is more heartbreaking? Who
has greater torments or more remorse?
Who has ever fallen farther or faster?

Great Oedipus, you emerged from birth's tight harbor,
and then returned there in your bridal bed
to make fast where your father had been before you.

SECOND CHORISTER
How could you plow that same furrow your father
sowed? How could it not cry out?
Time that sees all has found you out at last
and condemns your monstrous marriage that was no marriage
and produced your offspring who were not offspring.
Son of Laius, I wish I had never beheld you.

CHORUS
You restored us to life, or only a dream of life
we now lament sorely. From our lips
come only dirges. From you we drew our breath,
and now our eyes close as in sleep or death.

Exodos

[Enter SECOND MESSENGER]

SECOND MESSENGER
Elders of Thebes, you who have places of honor,
what horrors have I to tell you, what terrible actions
must I report for you to hear and endure.
If you have loyalty still to the house of Laius,
what mourning is in store for you. The mighty
Ister or Phasis could not wash this house clean,
such horrors are hidden inside, willed and unwilled.
And of all the griefs there are, none is more bitter
than what we contrive to bring down on ourselves.

FIRST CHORISTER
What we knew before was bad enough. What new
could add to that burden we already carry?

SECOND MESSENGER
My first piece of news is that Jocasta is dead.

SECOND CHORISTER
Oh, miserable! What caused it? How did she die?

SECOND MESSENGER
By her own hand. You are spared the worst of the pain
because you did not see it. But what I remember
I shall recount so that you may know.
When she left you to go inside, she went at once
to her bridal bed. She was tearing her hair out
with both hands. She slammed the doors behind her,
and called upon Laius, her dead husband, to wail
about how their making love in that very chamber
had brought him death and her a cursed offspring.
She wept upon that bed of misery where with her husband
she had brought forth another husband, and children
by her own child.
                              What happened then I cannot
say, for that was when Oedipus came in,
crying aloud and wandering aimlessly,
demanding from us a sword, and asking for her,
not calling her his wife but only the field
that had yielded two harvests, himself and his children.
And in his inspired fury, some god told him
where she was—for none of us had spoken—
and he rushed to the bedroom as if guided there,
broke down the doors, forcing the bolts inward

Her life back coming before her eyes

from their sockets, and then he fell into the room. *The rope, crashing through the chamber.*
There, we saw her, hanging from a noose.

　　Ah, and then the poor man groaned aloud
and he undid the knot and lay her down.
But then he took the pair of golden brooches
she wore upon her gown and raised his face
and thrust them into his eyes, saying that they
should not see how he suffered or what he had done
but, from now on, only stare at the darkness.
He would not look again upon those he should never
have seen, or recognize those he should never
have wanted to know. Saying such words as these,
he struck his bleeding eyeballs again and again,
and the blood ran down his cheeks and the drops of gore
spattered the floor like hail coming down from the sky.

　　That was how it ended, not with one person
suffering but the whole house, man and woman.
They had been happy and now all joy was gone,
supplanted by ruin and shame, pain and death.
What misery has mankind ever named
that they have not experienced today?

SECOND CHORISTER
And what does the wretched man plan to do now?

SECOND MESSENGER
He is calling out for the doors to be unbarred
so he can show all of Thebes his father's killer
and his mother's . . . No, I cannot say the word.
He means to banish himself. He will not stay
in this house in which he himself was the curse.
But he needs a guide, for he is too sick in body

and spirit to travel alone and to bear his griefs.
But you shall see, for he means to display himself
and you will witness what must move any man—
even one who hates him—to pity. See!

[OEDIPUS enters, blinded, his face bloodied.]

FIRST CHORISTER
What a terrible thing for men to behold. How awful!
I've never seen anything anywhere near so dreadful.
What madness seized you, miserable man?
What god has fallen upon you from a height
greater than great? Omoi! Omoi! Poor man!

SECOND CHORISTER
Poor man! I cannot bear to look at you.
I have questions that I am afraid to ask,
and answers I want, but . . . Horrible! Horrible.

OEDIPUS
Aieee! Where am I? In my pain,
where am I being carried? My voice goes out
into the air, but where? Oh, god, oh, god!
From how far you have leapt to land on my head?

FIRST CHORISTER
It's terrible! How can we bear to look at him?

OEDIPUS
Darkness, black, unbroken, irresistible
darkness, like that other unspeakable darkness
that followed me, sped by an evil wind. Omoi!
The bite of the gods' goad has sunk in my flesh
to remind me of my misery forever.

SECOND CHORISTER
It is hardly surprising that, burdened by such sorrows,
you should lament this way in doubled keening.

OEDIPUS
Oh, my friends.
You are still here to protect the poor blind man.
I cannot see your faces but in the dark
I know your voices. Ohhhh!

FIRST CHORISTER
You have done many terrible things, but this?
How did you bring yourself to blind yourself?
What god set you on this way?

OEDIPUS
                                    It was Apollo.
Apollo drove me to this, my friends, to these cruel
torments. But it was my own two hands,
my miserable hands that struck at my eyes.
If there was nothing I could look at with pleasure,
why look at all, ever?

FIRST CHORISTER
                                    I can see that.

OEDIPUS
What was I to look at that I could love?
What greeting could I hear? What familiar scene
could I pass by without the direst pain?
Take me away from here, my friends. I am lost,
utterly lost, cursed, and of all mortals,
the one the gods have hated most.

SECOND CHORISTER
                                        Wretched
in mind, and fortune, and now in your body also.
I wish that I had never even met you.

OEDIPUS
A curse upon that sentimental shepherd
who undid the fetters that bound my ankles and saved me
from death, preserving me for worse than death.
If I had died then, we'd be better off.

FIRST CHORISTER
It's sad, sad, but one cannot disagree.

OEDIPUS
I would not have survived to kill my father.
No one would call me my own mother's bridegroom.
I'm abandoned by the gods. I have defiled
my parents. If there is evil beyond evil,
that is the lot of Oedipus.

FIRST CHORISTER
It's a desperate choice you have made. You would have been better
dead than living as you've lived and are living now,
in blindness.

OEDIPUS
                    I don't want any advice or consolation.
There isn't anything anyone can say.
I could have killed myself, but then I thought
how can I look at my father's face in Hades?
How can I face my unhappy mother there?
I have done to each of them what cannot be
punished enough.

But here, in the light, how could I
bear to see my children, knowing who
they are and how they came into the world?
To look at them would have been an exquisite pain.
But then, even to see the city's walls,
the statues and the temples of the gods
in the city where I lived in such comfort and honor
and from which I am now cut off, cast out,
and, by my own lips, exiled, that pollution,
that killer of Laius who was of the race of Laius,
how could I think of it?
                              I was that blight, that stain,
and I could not gaze with steady eyes upon
those images I loved that now despise me.
Had I been able also to block my hearing
and be deaf as well as blind, I'd have done that too
to make a perfect cocoon for my wretchedness
where I could hide in my thoughts in a world of sorrow.
          Cithaeron, why did you cradle me, keeping me safe?
Why did you not show me the greater mercy
and kill me so that I could not reveal to my fellowman who I was and where I had come from?
O Polybus, o Corinth, you covered over
the sickness I carried inside me, and made me think
that I was at home in the lovely land of my fathers.
But the secret is out, and the evil expresses itself,
evil sprung from evil, continuing evil.
Cursed crossroads, cursed glade and narrow track,
where I shed my father's blood that was my blood
with my own cursed hands, do you still remember
the horror that happened there and the evil I did
when I was among you? Oh, and the marriage that gave me

birth and gave them the seeds of their deaths, a father
who was a brother, children who were the product
of incest, a bride who was also her husband's mother . . .
        But it is bad to speak of such bad things.
Lock me away somewhere. Kill me. Throw me
into the sea. Send me away where you'll never
see me again. You hate to touch me, but point me
where I must go. Do not be afraid. I am not
contagious, or not anymore. No one can bear
my woes but me.

[Enter CREON.]

FIRST CHORISTER
                But here, Creon is coming.
He will decide what to do, for no one is left
but him to take your place as the country's leader.

OEDIPUS
Omoi! What can I say to him? How can I hope
that he will listen to me. I've treated him badly,
suspecting him, accusing him . . . I was wrong.

CREON
I have not come to reproach you, Oedipus. Wrongs
you may have done in the past, we can forget.
But if you are shameless before your fellowman,
at least show respect for the Sun that nourishes all
and do not let it look down on such pollution.
The earth detests it, the sacred rain hates it,
the light of day itself recoils from it.

[To a SERVANT]
Take him into the house at once and hide him.
Piety demands that only his kinsmen
should see him or hear his sorrows.

OEDIPUS

                                    Creon, I beg you!
You have come in goodness to see my badness.
But grant me a favor I ask not for my sake
but rather for yours.

CREON

                    And what is this thing you want?

OEDIPUS
Cast me out of this land as soon as you can
to a place where I do not hear a human voice.

CREON
I would have done so already, but I am waiting
to hear from the voice of the god what he wants me to do.

OEDIPUS
The god has already spoken. He wants the impious
killer of Laius killed.

CREON

                    Such things were said,
but circumstances are different now and we ought
to find out exactly what is required of us.

OEDIPUS
You will ask the god what to do about this wretch?

CREON
Yes, and perhaps this time you'll believe what he says.

OEDIPUS
I will. But what I urge you to do is to bury
her, in the house, performing your duty as kinsman.
I know that you'll do what's right. And for me, exile.
You can't let me stay here in the city. Allow me
to go to Mount Cithaeron, where my mother
and father sent me. It was to be my tomb.
Let me seek there the death they wanted for me.
          One thing is clear to me now. I was preserved
from sickness or accident for a greater evil.
As for my children, don't worry about the boys,
who can fend for themselves and contrive to make their way.
But the poor dear girls, who ate at table with me,
take care of them. And let me, before I go,
touch them and lament with them for my sorrows.
Creon, your blood is noble, and I appeal
to your generosity—let me caress them again,
and let me feel their presence as I once did
when I could see.

[Enter ANTIGONE and ISMENE.]
          But what do I hear? They are weeping.
Creon has taken pity on me and brought them
here, my two dear children? Am I right?

CREON
Yes, you are correct. I know the joy
you used to take from having them near you.

OEDIPUS

I wish you good fortune—and may the gods give you
better protection and guidance than what I had.
Children, where are you? Come here to your brother
and father, and let these hands serve in my blindness
—and I was always blind—for my poor eyes.

       I cannot see you but I can weep for you
as I imagine the bitter lives that await you
and think how men will treat you. Where will you go,
to what assemblies, feasts, or celebrations
will you be welcomed? You will return in tears
from the slights and insults you have had to endure.
And when you are of marriageable age,
who will be so brave as to risk the reproaches
he can be sure will come with such a match,
given your family history? What pain,
what misery will fail to attend upon you?
Your father killed his father, married his mother,
and begot you from the source of his own life.
Such are the cruel taunts that you will hear,
a vile continual drone! What groom would dare
defy them to marry you? No one. No one.
You will die childless, husbandless, loveless . . .

[To CREON.]
Son of Menoeceus, you are left
as the only father these girls have, their parents
having perished and being about to perish.
Acting as their father, do not look on
to see them wander begging and without husbands.
Do not degrade them to my abysmal condition,

but pity them, for they are deserving of pity,
having been deprived at their tender age
of everything except what your kindness gives them.
Nod your assent and touch them with your hand
as noble men touch suppliants.

[To the DAUGHTERS.]

And you, children,
if you were old enough and could understand,
I would give you words of advice. As it is,
all I can tell you is that you should pray,
for my sake, for better lives than your father had.
May you live wherever you can, as well as you can.

CREON
You have wept enough. Go inside, if you please.

OEDIPUS
I shall obey, but it does not at all please.

CREON
All things that are in season are right and proper.

OEDIPUS
Do you know on what condition I'll go inside?

CREON
I expect that you are about to let me know.

OEDIPUS
That you send me out of the country.

CREON

What you ask

is in the gift of the gods.

OEDIPUS

But the gods detest me.

CREON

If so, that gift will be sooner rather than later.

OEDIPUS

Do you think so?

CREON

That's what I just said.

You know me. I don't speak lightly or joke.

OEDIPUS

Take me away.

CREON

Go, and let go of your children.

OEDIPUS

No, no, don't take them from me.

CREON

Still giving orders?

Even when you had control, you did not

have control, but only supposed so.

[CREON, OEDIPUS, and the DAUGHTERS exit into the palace.]

FIRST CHORISTER

Men of Thebes, see what a rain of catastrophes
comes on Oedipus here. He answered the Sphinx's
riddle and he was the man to whom we turned
in admiration and envy. Look at him now.

SECOND CHORISTER

Call none among mortals fortunate until
he has passed on without grief from this dangerous world.

Play emphasizes Oedipus' desire
to see the truth at last.
You may discover horrors, but
owning the horrors "This is me."
Apollo ordained
but the hand that struck his eyes
Here is the humanism
accept the past & act on it
Pursuit of the truth
"I did it all myself."
It's mine alone
My destiny
He is fashioning his life —
Form of mastery — shaping his
life.

Oedipus at Colonus

Dramatis Personae

OEDIPUS	formerly king of Thebes
ANTIGONE	daughter of Oedipus and Jocasta
ISMENE	daughter of Oedipus and Jocasta
STRANGER	a stranger to Oedipus, a resident of Colonus
CHORUS	of elders
CREON	ruler of Thebes, and Oedipus's brother-in-law
THESEUS	king of Athens
POLYNEICES	son of Oedipus and Jocasta
MESSENGER	

Silent Roles

SOLDIERS	of Theseus and of Creon
ATTENDANT	of Ismene

Prologue

[A rural setting near the grove of the Eumenides at Colonus. In center stage is a rock that can be used as a seat. There is also a semicircular ridge of low rocks on the edge of which people can sit. There is a statue of Colonus, the dead hero. OEDIPUS and ANTIGONE enter.]

OEDIPUS
Antigone, child of an old blind man, where are we?
What place is this? What city of men have we come to?
Who now shall welcome wandering Oedipus
who brings but scanty gifts? Expecting little,
I get even less, but that, for me, is enough,
for suffering and time that have been my companions
have instructed me in contentment. Nobility, too,
teaches me patience.
                          But child, do you see a place
where I can stop and sit down, somewhere safe,
neither forbidden to strangers nor consecrated?
Perhaps some temple park would do. Lead me
there and let me rest. We can find out
where we are. Having come as strangers,
we must learn from the citizens what their customs are
and what we must do to conform and show respect.

ANTIGONE
Unhappy Oedipus, there are city walls
in the distance. But I'd guess where we are is sacred—
there are olives, bays, and vines everywhere, and the music
of nightingales. Rest your weary legs. I see
a rock where you can sit down. You've traveled a long
way, for an old man.

OEDIPUS

                    Help me sit down.
And keep watch, as I can't do.

ANTIGONE

                              Yes, I know.
I know. After all this time, you don't have to tell me.

[She seats OEDIPUS on the rock at center stage.]

OEDIPUS

Can you tell me where we are?

ANTIGONE

                              Outside of Athens.
But I don't know what they call this particular place.

OEDIPUS

That's what the people we met on the road said.

ANTIGONE

Shall I go and try to find out where we are?

OEDIPUS

Yes, my child. And ask if one can live here.

ANTIGONE

Well, people do live here. But I don't need
to go far. I can see a man nearby.

OEDIPUS

Is he coming toward us?

[Enter STRANGER]

ANTIGONE
                    No, he's already here,
close enough to ask him whatever you like.

OEDIPUS
Stranger, this girl whose eyes serve me and herself
tells me that you have appeared at the right moment
to answer the questions we have . . .

STRANGER
                                        Before you ask them,
leave that seat. You are on holy ground,
where no one may set foot without pollution.

OEDIPUS
What is this place, then? To which of the gods is it sacred?

STRANGER
Nobody lives here. This forbidden place is owned
by the dread goddesses, daughters of Earth and Night.

OEDIPUS
And by what solemn name does one address them?

STRANGER
The people around here call them the all-seeing
Eumenides, the gentle ones. There are other
names that people use in other places.

OEDIPUS
May they receive in good grace and in pity
a suppliant, for I'll never leave this seat.

STRANGER
But, sir, what do you mean?

OEDIPUS
                              This place is fated.

STRANGER
I can't order you to leave, but I must report
back to the city that you are here.

OEDIPUS
                              Bear with me,
stranger. I am an old vagrant, but answer
my questions, I beg you.

STRANGER
                    Ask whatever you like.

OEDIPUS
What is the name of this place that we have entered?

STRANGER
I shall tell you what I know. All of this place
is sacred. It belongs to the great Poseidon,
and the fire-bearing Titan Prometheus also
dwells here. The spot where you walk we call the Bronze
Threshold. It is Athens' holy bulwark,
and the country around us takes its name from Colonus,
the horseman whose statue is there. That is the story,
a little story perhaps, but we who live here
believe in it and honor it in our hearts.

OEDIPUS
So there are people who live around here?

STRANGER

Yes,
and they take the name of the town from that of the god.

OEDIPUS
Is there a ruler? Or do they rule themselves?

STRANGER
The place is ruled by a king who lives in the city.

OEDIPUS
His power comes from his eloquence and strength?

STRANGER
His name is Theseus, son of King Aegeus.

OEDIPUS
And could you send a messenger to him?

STRANGER
Do you want to send a message? To prepare him?

OEDIPUS
A small favor to me could earn him much.

STRANGER
What help can the king expect from a blind old man?

OEDIPUS
The words that I shall utter will have sight.

STRANGER
Stranger, I do not mean you harm. You look
noble, judging from your manner, although
your present fortune hardly comports with that.

But stay here where you are, and I shall speak
to the men of the neighborhood rather than those in the city—
and leave it to them to decide if you may stay
or must move on again.

[Exit STRANGER.]

OEDIPUS

Child, has he left?

ANTIGONE
He has, father. You can relax and say
whatever you like. There's no one here but us.

OEDIPUS

[Praying to the Eumenides.]
Dames of dread aspect, I have arrived
at a place sacred to you, having been drawn
hither. Show respect to Apollo and pity
for me, for when that god predicted evils
that would befall me, he said that this would be
my place of respite after many long years,
when I came to take shelter here in the seat
of the awesome goddesses. Here I would reach the goal
of my long-suffering life. And here, somehow,
I would bring benefit to those who received me
kindly and ruin to those who drove me away.
He said there would be signs and omens, earthquakes,
or the thunder and lightning of Zeus. I have trusted in this,
and you have brought me here to this sacred grove
leading my way. I come, a sober man,
to invoke the goddesses for whom libations

are water, milk, and honey, to take my seat
on this unhewn rock of yours. Goddesses, come,
as Apollo said you would, and grant a passage
that will end the troubled life of Fortune's slave
and sufferings such as no man has ever known.
Come, sweet daughters of darkness. And Athens, hear me,
honored city of great Pallas Athena,
take pity on this sad ghost of a man,
which is all that remains of what was once Oedipus.

ANTIGONE
Hush, father. Some old men are approaching.

OEDIPUS
I shall be still. But hide me in the grove,
and let us exercise caution and hear what they say.

[ANTIGONE leads OEDIPUS off, left.]

Parodos

[The CHORUS of elders enters from the right.]

FIRST CHORISTER
Look! Where is he? Who is he?

SECOND CHORISTER
                              Has he gone?

THIRD CHORISTER
Blasphemous! Outrageous!

FIRST CHORISTER
Not from here!
Some stranger, some hobo. Wicked, or maybe
ignorant—to enter the sacred grove
of these dread virgins we dare not name!

SECOND CHORISTER
We pass them
with lowered eyes, in silence, in respect.
But someone has marched boldly into this place
utterly lacking in reverence, or even defiant . . .

SECOND CHORISTER
I've looked all around and I see no trace of him.

[OEDIPUS reveals himself, reentering from the left.]

OEDIPUS
I am the one you are looking for. It's me.
I see, as blind men are said to do, with my ears.

SECOND CHORISTER
Oh, terrible! To look at him and to hear him!

OEDIPUS
I'm not an outlaw. Do not be afraid.

FIRST CHORISTER
Protector Zeus! Who is this old man?

OEDIPUS
No one
to be afraid of, and certainly no one to envy.
Guardians of this land, consider my plight

as I move along, using another's eyes,
an old man leaning on a youngster's shoulders.

FIRST CHORISTER
Were you blind from birth? Your life has been a sad one,
or so one would assume.

SECOND CHORISTER
                              But still, there are limits,
and what you do is not permitted. Never!
You bring down a curse on us all by what you do,
entering this glade and breaking its silence.
This is a holy place where the honey drips
into the spring-fed bowl!

THIRD CHORISTER
                              Stand back, stand back!
It is forbidden ground. Do you understand?
Keep away, for the gods' sake! And our own.

FIRST CHORISTER
Your condition is heartbreaking, and yet you must heed
our cautions! If you have something to say to us,
move from that forbidden place. Then speak.

OEDIPUS
Daughter, what should we do?

ANTIGONE
                              We must respect
these citizens and give way to them.

OEDIPUS
                              Lead me.

ANTIGONE
Here is my hand. Take it.

OEDIPUS
                              Gentlemen, see,
I trust you. Do me no harm. I am moving.

[OEDIPUS leaves the rock and comes downstage.]

THIRD CHORISTER
No one will hurt you or move you against your will.

OEDIPUS
Is this far enough?

SECOND CHORISTER
                    A little further.

OEDIPUS
                                        Enough?

FIRST CHORISTER
You can see, young woman. A little more.

ANTIGONE
It's all right, father. Follow where I lead.[1]

SECOND CHORISTER
You are a stranger in a strange land, poor man.
You must learn to hate what our city hates and show
the proper respect to those things it respects.

OEDIPUS
Daughter, lead me the right way so that I step
where piety says it is proper and allowed.
We must listen to others and yield to necessity's dictates.

[Slowly and carefully, ANTIGONE leads OEDIPUS to the circular
ledge that demarcates the grove.]

ANTIGONE
Here. Be careful, there's a ledge of rock. Stop here.

OEDIPUS
Like this?

THIRD CHORISTER
                          Yes, that's far enough.

OEDIPUS
                                                    May I sit?

THIRD CHORISTER
Yes, to your side, crouch down. There's a low ledge.

ANTIGONE
Let me help you father. It's just behind you.

OEDIPUS

[Bumping himself and in pain.]
Oh! Omoi!

ANTIGONE
Yes, lean on me. You're there. Sit, sit.

OEDIPUS

[Sitting.]
Oh, ah. This miserable blindness!

FIRST CHORISTER
Unhappy man, now that you're comfortable, tell us
who you are, led thus in such pain?
What country do you call your fatherland?

OEDIPUS
Strangers, I am an exile, but do not ask . . .

SECOND CHORISTER
What do you want us not to ask, old man?

OEDIPUS
Don't ask me who I am. No more questions, please.

THIRD CHORISTER
Why not?

OEDIPUS
                    My birth was . . . terrible.

FIRST CHORISTER
                                        What do you mean?

OEDIPUS
My child, my child. What am I to say?

FIRST CHORISTER
Tell us what seed you come from? Who was your father?

OEDIPUS
Oh, daughter. What will happen to me now?

SECOND CHORISTER
You seem to be driven to the brink. Tell us.

OEDIPUS
Very well, I will speak. I'm afraid I cannot hide it.

THIRD CHORISTER
Hide it or delay it further. Speak!

OEDIPUS
Have you heard of a son of Laius?

CHORUS
                                        Ohhh! Ohhh!

OEDIPUS
And the house of Labdacus?

CHORUS
                                        Ohhh! Oh, Zeus!

OEDIPUS
The unhappy Oedipus?

FIRST CHORISTER
                          And you are he?

OEDIPUS
Don't be afraid of what I say.

FIRST CHORISTER
                          Oh! Oh!

OEDIPUS
Miserable!

SECOND CHORISTER
                    Oh! Oh!

OEDIPUS

[To ANTIGONE]
                    What will happen now?

FIRST CHORISTER
Go. You must go. Far away from our country.

OEDIPUS
But you promised! Are you not men of your word?

FIRST CHORISTER
If we were deceitful, you were deceitful first.
Fate does not punish those who fight back when attacked,
giving pain for pain. You must go away,
hurry from our country, and leave us alone
lest for your sake we suffer some heavy burden.

ANTIGONE
Strangers, you are honorable men.
I know that you all know his sorry story
and understand that those things that my father
did unwittingly trouble you, and yet
I ask you—I beseech you—pity me
when I appeal to you on my father's behalf.
I look into your eyes with my own eyes
that are not blind, and ask, as if I were
the child of one of you, for pity, for mercy

for this beaten man who ought to have some respect.
We are in your hands and we pray as if to gods
that you are somehow moved to grant us your favor.
Think of what you love—a child, a wife,
some treasure, or some god. And then think of this,
that you can never, no matter how hard you may look
in all the world, find a mortal anywhere
who can escape the fury of heaven and of fate.

Scene I

FIRST CHORISTER
Daughter of Oedipus, we do pity him
and you as well for your unfortunate fortune,
but we fear what may come upon us from the gods
if we dare some other answer to your request.

OEDIPUS
Everyone knows Athens' great reputation
for reverence for the gods and for how they treat
afflicted strangers, but what does that turn out to be?
Empty talk! Look at my sorry case
and what you have done and are making me do now,
driving me away in fear of my name.
It isn't me you're afraid of, a blind old man,
or what I did, which was only to suffer.

                                    I'd tell you
the story, my mother's, my father's, and mine, but know
I never intended evil. I was struck
and I struck back, as almost anyone would.
And I came to Thebes not knowing who I was,

or who my parents were, and the world used me
terribly, and I was destroyed. As you see.
　　　Because of all this, I implore you, strangers,
as a stranger here and in reverence for the gods,
that you grant me refuge. The gods look down and see
what men do, the good whom they reward
and the bad whom they harry and punish, and no one escapes.
I ask you to follow their guidance and for your sakes
not to becloud the fame of fortunate Athens.
Receive the honest suppliant, protect me,
and do not dishonor me or turn away
from my ugliness. I come in holiness
and bring advantage to all citizens here.
When he who is your leader comes to hear me,
he shall know all, but till then, do not be wicked.

FIRST CHORISTER
What you have said, old man, we regard with awe,
for your words are grave indeed, and I am content
to leave this matter to our country's rulers.

OEDIPUS
And where, sir, is the ruler of this land?

SECOND CHORISTER
He is in our parent city. The man who brought us
here has hurried on to Athens to fetch him.

OEDIPUS
Will he come all this way and concern himself
with the plight of an old blind man?

THIRD CHORISTER

When he hears your name,
be assured, he will come.

OEDIPUS

Who will bring this message?

FIRST CHORISTER

Who will not? The talk of travelers carried
your history far and wide. Were he lazy and slow,
he'd hasten here to see you and hear what you say.

OEDIPUS

I hope he may be repaid and his coming here
may bring good fortune both to me and the city—
for the deeds of noble men do good for themselves.

ANTIGONE

Oh, Zeus! I can't believe it! I dare not. Father?

OEDIPUS

What is it, my child?

ANTIGONE

I see a woman approaching.
She's riding a Sicilian pony and wearing
one of those broad-brimmed sunhats of the kind
they wear in Thessaly. I can't see her face.
And I can't trust my guess, which prompts one way
and then another, and I think I'm being foolish,
hoping and fearing at once, but, yes, she's waving,
and smiling, I think. It has to be Ismene!

OEDIPUS
What? What did you say?

ANTIGONE
                                That I see my sister,
your daughter Ismene. And soon we'll hear her voice!

[Enter ISMENE and a SERVANT.]

ISMENE
Father, sister! How good it is to see you.
Looking for you has been hard, and now I must say
looking at you is also hard. My heart
breaks for you both.

OEDIPUS
                        My child, is it you?

ISMENE
                                        Oh, father!
What a pathetic sight you are.
                                ·
OEDIPUS
                                Ismene,
you've appeared!

ISMENE
                    It wasn't easy. But, yes, I have.

OEDIPUS
Touch me, my daughter.

ISMENE
                    I touch you both, together.

OEDIPUS
Ah, my children. My sisters.

ISMENE
                              Unhappy together.

OEDIPUS
Do you mean her and me?

ISMENE
                              Yes, but me, too.

OEDIPUS
Why have you come, child?

ISMENE
                              I was worried about you.

OEDIPUS
You missed me?

ISMENE
                    Yes, but I also have some news.
I came with the only trustworthy servant I have.

OEDIPUS
But what about your brothers? Do they not take
their share of our burden of troubles?

ISMENE
                                        They are where they are.
Their situation is grim.

OEDIPUS

Those two have adopted
the Egyptian style, I'm afraid. There, men are at home,
weaving and doing the housework, while the women
are outside in the world earning a living.
Here you are and your sister, who ought to be home,
safe somewhere, and doing what good girls do,
helping with the household affairs, but instead
you two are here with me, to help your unhappy
father bear his terrible sorrows. One
has wandered with me, poor thing, and cared for me,
a young girl who herself ought to be cared for.
She was barely strong enough to make this journey
but has helped me, feeble and old as I am, lending
me her strength of will. Together we've crossed
trackless wilderness, having no food, with nothing
to wear on our feet, nothing to keep the drenching
rains from soaking our bodies or the scorching
sun from baking down on our bare heads.
And all this time, the poor dear girl who should
be safe at home is with me, caring for me,
and always thinking of me before herself.
And you, my child, have come to us before,
secretly, so that no one in Thebes knew,
to let me know the prophecies you had heard
concerning me. I had been sent into exile,
but you were my faithful agent still, my loyal
friend. And what is it now? What news do you bring?
What prompts your coming, Ismene? I am certain
that you have not journeyed this far from home without
reason or empty-handed. Should I be afraid?

ISMENE

The troubles I've had on the road in search of you two
I shall not bother to detail. It is painful
to think of them again. The news I bring
is not of my own tribulations but those of your
unhappy sons. At first, they agreed that Creon
should have the throne, our ancient and ruined family's
sorry plight being what it is, for the sake
of the city and to keep our pollution from it.
But some malign god has inspired these
thrice-miserable brothers to vie for power,
each reaching for dominion and the throne.
Eteocles, the younger one, now holds it
and has sent his elder brother, Polyneices,
out of the country. The story I hear is that now
he is in low-lying Argos, and has married.
He is recruiting friends to join with him
in arms to recover Thebes for himself or else
seek a place in heaven. I wish it were only
a story, but it's true and dreadful. When
will the gods at last take pity on your sorrows?

OEDIPUS

You have persuaded yourself that the gods pay any
attention to me at all?

ISMENE

                  Yes, father, they do,
according to the latest prophecy.

OEDIPUS

                        What
prophecy do you mean? What does it say?

ISMENE
That our people shall have need of you and seek
your help both before your death and afterwards, too.

OEDIPUS
What kind of help could they expect from me?

ISMENE
It says the city's power depends on you.

OEDIPUS
Even after I no longer exist?

ISMENE
Yes. The gods who once destroyed you will now
somehow lift you up.

OEDIPUS
                              It's irrelevant now
to lift me up, old and feeble, after
contriving my terrible fall when I was young.

ISMENE
Because of this oracle, Creon will be coming
to ask your help. And it will be soon.

OEDIPUS
                                        What
on earth can he possibly want from me?

ISMENE
                                        He wants
that you should live somewhere just beyond the border,
not quite in Thebes but where they can control you.

OEDIPUS
But what help do they think I can do them there?

ISMENE
They worry about your tomb, which could cause them trouble.

OEDIPUS
Ah, even without the word of the god, one might
have guessed it would be something like that.

ISMENE
                                        That's why
they want you near them, where you cannot be
your own master.

OEDIPUS
                        Will my body have Theban soil?

ISMENE
The shedding of your kindred's blood forbids that.

OEDIPUS
Then they shall never have power over me.

ISMENE
The Thebans will be worried.

OEDIPUS
                                Why? What
would they worry about?

ISMENE
                        That a day may come when they stand
where you are buried and feel the heat of your anger.

OEDIPUS
Who told you that?

ISMENE
                    The men who had gone to Delphi.

OEDIPUS
And this is what Apollo said? Of me?

ISMENE
That's what they said when they returned to Thebes.

OEDIPUS
Did either one of my sons hear about this?

ISMENE
Both of them, father. Each of them knows.

OEDIPUS
                                        And still,
each is after the throne and wants that more
than to be with me again?

ISMENE
                        It is painful to hear
you say this, but that's how it is. I can't deny it.

OEDIPUS
I ask the gods to keep their quarrel alive
but not them. Let them both wield their spears,
so that the one who holds the throne dies
and the other, who has gone off, never returns.
I remember how, when I was expelled from the city,
neither one of them raised a hand to prevent it

or defend his father. They stood there in silent assent.
It wasn't what I'd wanted, you remember.
My passions were blazing then and, in my distress,
I asked to be stoned to death, brutal and quick,
but nobody came forward to grant my wish.
In time, my spirit's terrible pain diminished.
My rage began to subside and I understood
I had been too harsh with myself about my errors.
And then? Did they help me at all? Did they show the concern
dutiful sons owe a father? No!
These two, my daughters, gave me that help a blind
old man relies on, wandering endless roads
of exile. From them I had food, clothing, protection . . .
My sons were too busy squabbling over a scepter
to give any thought to me. And they shall get nothing
now from me in return. That throne of Thebes
that once was mine shall do them no good. I know this
from what Ismene reports of Apollo's decree.

      Therefore, strangers, I say let Creon come,
or anyone else from that city. If you are willing,
and if these awesome goddesses are willing
to give me sanctuary, you will enjoy
my protection and see your enemies suffer!

FIRST CHORISTER
You deserve compassion, Oedipus, you
and your two daughters as well. You offer protection,
and I reciprocate with some helpful advice.

OEDIPUS
Speak, good host. Be an ally now
and I will accomplish much for you, someday.

FIRST CHORISTER
You have walked on holy ground. I recommend
you perform therefore the rite of purification.

OEDIPUS
And what would that entail?

FIRST CHORISTER
                              You must bring libations
from the sacred and ever-flowing crystal stream,
and your hands that touch them must be clean.

OEDIPUS
                                                      And then?
When I have this untainted libation, what do I do?

FIRST CHORISTER
You will find basins, the work of excellent craftsmen.
Deck their rims and the handles on both sides.

OEDIPUS
With olive or laurel branches? With woolen cloths?

FIRST CHORISTER
With the newly sheared fleece of a young lamb.

OEDIPUS
Very well, and what do I do then?

FIRST CHORISTER
At the first light of dawn, you must pour your libation.

OEDIPUS
With these bowls that you have mentioned before?

FIRST CHORISTER

                                                     Yes,

in three streams, and the last one you empty out.

OEDIPUS

What goes into the bowls?

FIRST CHORISTER

                          Honey and water.

But no wine.

OEDIPUS

                 And then? When the earth has received this?

FIRST CHORISTER

Place thrice nine twigs of olive and say these prayers . . .

OEDIPUS

Wait. Speak clearly. I want to get it right.

FIRST CHORISTER

Pray that as we call them the kindly ones,
the Eumenides, that they may be pleased to receive
with kindly hearts a suppliant and protect him.
You or anyone acting on your behalf
must ask this, speaking softly and with respect.
No raised voices or crying aloud. And then
depart backing up, without turning around.
If you do this, I am with you. But if not,
then I'm afraid of what will become of you.

OEDIPUS

Daughters, you hear the words of the helpful stranger?

ISMENE
We have listened, father. What shall we do?

OEDIPUS
I cannot go, myself. I have not the strength
and I cannot see. One of you must go
to perform the rite for the three of us as he
prescribed. Even one, who is sincere, may speak
for a larger number. One of you, go. The other
must stay with me here to help me and be my guide.

ISMENE
I will go and perform the rite. But where?

FIRST CHORISTER
On the other side of the grove. And if you should need
help, there is an attendant there to instruct you.

ISMENE
I will go at once. Antigone, you stay here
to take care of father. The trouble one must take
for the sake of a parent, one doesn't remember as trouble.

[ISMENE exits.]

Ode I

FIRST CHORISTER
It is an awesome thing to reawaken
ancient evils, stranger, but I long
to learn . . .

OEDIPUS
What?

FIRST CHORISTER
Of those pains from which you suffered.

OEDIPUS
In the name of the sacred bond between host and guest,
I beg you not to reopen those old wounds.

SECOND CHORISTER
Your story is everywhere and people tell
various versions. We wish to hear the truth.

OEDIPUS
Omoi!

THIRD CHORISTER
Be patient with us, sir, I do entreat you.

OEDIPUS
Ohhhh! Ohhhh!

FIRST CHORISTER
Trust us. We have given you all you have asked.

OEDIPUS
I endured evil, strangers. I did not cause it
but by the gods and my own will I endured it.

FIRST CHORISTER
What do you mean?

OEDIPUS
                        It was the wicked marriage
the city condemned me to and, ignorant, I
agreed to it. My ruin came from that.

SECOND CHORISTER
You mean you married your mother and shared her bed?

OEDIPUS
Omoi! It is death to me to hear this spoken,
but yes, and we produced these girls, my daughters . . .

THIRD CHORISTER
Yes, go on.

OEDIPUS
                        These two unfortunate girls!

SECOND CHORISTER
Oh, Zeus!

OEDIPUS
                Who were born from my own mother's womb.

FIRST CHORISTER
So they are both your daughters and your sisters?

OEDIPUS
Yes, they are their father's sisters.

CHORUS
                        Ahhhh!

OEDIPUS
The evils are endless and relentless.

FIRST CHORISTER
                                        You
have suffered . . .

OEDIPUS
                              Yes. Unbelievable woe.

FIRST CHORISTER
You sinned.

OEDIPUS
                    No, I did not!

THIRD CHORISTER
                              How can you say that?

OEDIPUS
I won her as a prize for the service I'd done
the city. How could I ever have suspected?

SECOND CHORISTER
It is also said in the stories we hear that you murdered . . .

OEDIPUS
What else do you want to know?

SECOND CHORISTER
                                        That you killed your father.

OEDIPUS
You have struck a terrible blow, a bruise on a bruise.

THIRD CHORISTER
You killed him.

OEDIPUS
                    Yes, yes, but let me explain . . .

SECOND CHORISTER
Explain what?

OEDIPUS
                    I did murder my father,
but I had no knowledge at all of who he was.
It was the gods who drove me to do this thing.
But under the law, I was ignorant. And guiltless.

[The CHORUS turns to look at stage right, from which THESEUS
is about to enter.]

Scene II

FIRST CHORISTER
Here he comes, Theseus, son of Aegeus,
our king, whom we have summoned at your request.

[Enter THESEUS and SOLDIERS.]

THESEUS
I heard long ago and from many men the account
of your bloody destruction of your eyes. It is easy
for me to recognize you, son of Laius.
If there were any question, your clothing, your face,
and your demeanor attest to who you are.
In pity, Oedipus, I ask what request you have

of me and of our city, you and your sad
companion here. Tell me what it might be,
and unless it spells ruin for all of us, I
promise I shall not deny you or turn away
from your plight. I was an exile once, and grew up
among dangers few men have ever imagined,
let alone known. How could I not be helpful
to a brother in exile? We mortals live uncertain
lives. No one can take tomorrow for granted.

OEDIPUS
Theseus, your noble words leave me
with no adequate answer. You are correct
about who I am, and who my father was,
and where I come from. All that remains is for me
to ask that you grant me what I desire.

THESEUS
                                              What?

OEDIPUS
I come to offer the unprepossessing gift
of this fragile body. But I do assure you, sir,
that benefits will accrue from your acceptance.

THESEUS
What benefits are these, if I may ask?

OEDIPUS
You will learn this in good time, but not quite yet.

THESEUS
When then will they be revealed?

OEDIPUS

        When I die,
and when you give me burial.

THESEUS

       When you die?
But what about the interval? Have you forgotten
that you are still alive? Or do you dismiss that?

OEDIPUS

Yes, because the benefits come with my death.

THESEUS

You are not asking for much, then.

OEDIPUS

        It's not so simple.

THESEUS

Do you refer to your sons?

OEDIPUS

       Yes, they will try
to force me to return to Thebes.

THESEUS

       If they want you,
it is not right for you to remain in exile.

OEDIPUS

When I wished to remain I could not. Now, they want me!

THESEUS
Are you not being foolish? You are in need,
and anger is unlikely to bring you advantage.

OEDIPUS
When I have told you everything, you may
criticize or reprove. Until then, patience.

THESEUS
That's true. I ought not to judge until I know more.

OEDIPUS
I have suffered, Theseus, wrongs on wrongs.

THESEUS
You refer to the house of Laius and its troubles?

OEDIPUS
No, everyone in Greece knows about that.

THESEUS
What greater affliction could there be than that?

OEDIPUS
Here is my dilemma. I killed my father
and was driven from my country by my children.
I can never go back there.

THESEUS
                              Then how could they bring you back?

OEDIPUS
The god will compel them to do this.

THESEUS

                              What disaster
do they seek to avoid by bringing you home now?

OEDIPUS
Their fate is to be struck down here, in this land.

THESEUS
We have no quarrel with them. What do you mean?

OEDIPUS
Beloved son of Aegeus, for the gods there is no
age or death. For the rest of us, relentless
time devours all. The strength of a country
like the strength of a human body grows and wanes.
The bonds of trust and loyalty fray and friendship
wears away—between men and between
cities, too, as happiness turns bitter.
Sometimes it may revive and sometimes not.
The weather now between you and Thebes is sunny,
but the skies change and weather can turn foul.
Over the course of countless days and nights
the pleasant pledges you and Thebes have exchanged
may shatter as spears are thrown for trivial reasons.
Then shall my sleeping corpse become your blessing
and, cold as it is, shall drink their too hot blood—
assuming only that Zeus is still Zeus and his son
Phoebus Apollo speaks the truth to us.
But these are painful subjects. Let us not
dwell upon them. All that is required
is that you keep your word, and you shall see
how Oedipus, whom you welcomed into this land,
was—if the gods do not tell lies—not useless.

SECOND CHORISTER
Lord, he has promised much, and we believe him.

THESEUS
Who could doubt such a man or reject his good will?
As I see it, he comes to us as an ally,
and our hearth should therefore be open to him in welcome.
Then, too, he comes as a suppliant of the gods,
and he offers me and our country no small reward
for granting him sanctuary. I must respect
each and all of these reasons and for his kindness
shall allow him to settle here and dwell among us.
Should he wish to remain here where he is in Colonus,
I shall appoint you to guard him and care for him.
Or, should he wish to come with me to Athens,
he may do that too. Whatever it is he chooses,
that he may have. And this is my public promise.

OEDIPUS
Oh Zeus, bless this man for his decency.

THESEUS
What is it that you wish? To come to the palace?

OEDIPUS
I would, but this is the place . . .

THESEUS
                              Where you will do what?

OEDIPUS
Where I shall triumph over those who threw me out.

THESEUS
We are grateful to you for the great gift of your presence.

OEDIPUS
It will bring you good, if you honor the pledge you made.

THESEUS
Do not be afraid. I shall never betray you.

OEDIPUS
I do not distrust you or ask for any oath.

THESEUS
An oath would be worth no more to you than my word.

OEDIPUS
How then will you fulfill this promise?

THESEUS
                                            What
is it that you most fear?

OEDIPUS
                              That men will come . . .

THESEUS
These gentlemen here will attend to them and protect you.

OEDIPUS
Be sure, when you leave me . . .

THESEUS
                              I do not need instructions!

OEDIPUS
I know. But I'm worried . . .

THESEUS
                              You may be. I'm not.

OEDIPUS
You don't know what the dangers are.

THESEUS
                                    I know
that no one shall carry you off against my will.
The air may be full of threats, but when the mind
is in control and steadies itself, they vanish.
They may have made proud noises about their plans,
but the sea they have to cross is more of a challenge
than they may expect, wider, rougher, and harder
to navigate. Be confident both in me
but also in Phoebus Apollo, who sent you here.
Know that whether or not I am here with you,
my name is enough to guard you from rough treatment.

[THESEUS and his SOLDIERS exit.]

Ode II

[The CHORUS addresses OEDIPUS.]

FIRST CHORISTER
We welcome you to Colonus, this paradise,
this country of fine horses, a poet's dream
of perfect beauty and ease where birdsong ever
bubbles out of the ivy and down from the leaves

of fruit trees that nod assent in a gentle wind.
Here, divine Dionysos dances in joy
and revels in the company of his Maenads.
It never rains, but the gentle dew descends
each morning to nourish clusters of bright narcissus
that crowned the goddess Demeter and her daughter
and bedazzle the gold of the crocus with fresh diamonds.
The clear brook that our river god has blessed
never runs dry but gentles the bosom of earth
with crystal water so that the chorus of Muses
idles here sometimes and Aphrodite
does not despise this place and its delights.

SECOND CHORISTER
Here we have something I have not heard of in Asia
or the Peloponnese where the Dorians live, a tree
planted by no man's hand that no man tames
even with hostile weapons. It flourishes here
with its gray-green leaves to nurture its children, the olives,
and it lives forever, astonishing the young
and giving the old comfort, for Zeus, all-seeing,
looks after it as does gray-eyed Athena.

THIRD CHORISTER
I too have praise for Athens, our mother-city,
that the generous god has blessed with the might of horses,
the strength of healthy foals, and the awesome power
of the sea, itself—I mean the son of Cronos
who enthroned our splendid city, Lord Poseidon.
He gave us bridles to tame quick-footed horses
and oars for the waves, the Nereids' countless feet.

Scene III

[ANTIGONE is looking off, stage right.]

ANTIGONE
A splendid and famous land, but now is the time
to demonstrate that these shining words are true.

OEDIPUS
What do you mean by that? What do you see?

ANTIGONE
Creon is approaching. With armed men.

OEDIPUS
Ah, elders, now is the time I need your protection.

FIRST CHORISTER
You have nothing to fear. We may be old, but the city
of Athens is young and strong, and unafraid.

[Enter CREON with SOLDIERS.]

CREON
Gentlemen, I see in your eyes concern—
I will not call it fear—but I assure you
my arrival here is no cause for alarm.
Let us be realists, after all. I am old
and know my limitations. This is as great
and powerful a city as any in Greece.
I do not come to menace you but persuade
this man to come with me back to the land of Thebes.
I am not sent by any single person
but I do the bidding of all the citizens there

who chose me for my family connection,
which causes me, after all, to mourn for his many
troubles more deeply than anyone at home.
           Come, Oedipus, listen to what I say.
The people of Cadmus' city summon you back.
And properly so, I believe, for if I am not
the worst of men, I must feel your pain, an old
blind man who wanders the earth in exile, poor
and with only the one attendant. . . . Never could I
have imagined that this girl could fall from such comfort
and prominence to this misery I see,
your body-servant, protector, and your guide.
At her age, to be living like a beggar,
without a husband, at the mercy of strangers and chance!
           I ask you, is this sad story not the truth?
It is a shame, for you, for me, and for all
the family! In the name of your father's gods,
I ask you to yield to my words and return
to the home of your ancestors, thanking these good people
and this fair city, which has treated you well,
but still is not your home. And in all justice
and piety, that is where you belong, in Thebes,
where you were born so many years ago.

OEDIPUS
Shameless man! You will stop at nothing! Your plea
is utterly transparent, a cunning scheme
to catch me in your trap and cause me pain!
When I was suffering my private grief
and wished to be sent away from the city, you
prevented me from going. Then, when my grief
subsided and I said I'd prefer to remain at home,

you were the one who drove me into exile.
Where was that family feeling then, that kinship
you boast about? And now, when I've found at last
a kindly city willing to take me in,
you come with your harsh thoughts dressed in the softest
words to tear me away! Do you enjoy this?
You like being kind to people against their will?
Can you imagine how it feels when someone
gives you nothing when you are in dire need
and are begging for a crust of bread, but later,
when your fortunes have improved and you've had your fill,
offers to buy you dinner? What unkind kindness!
That's why your offer now seems like an insult
or even a blow, for all your high-flown talk.
You and I know the lay of the land, but these men
perhaps need some explanation to understand
what a villain you are! You come to invite me home
not out of any compassion but only to keep me
somewhere out near the border for the protection
of Thebes someday against the city of Athens.
You shall not have it. What you shall have is this—
that I shall stay here and hate you, and my spirit
will hate you forever. And as for my sons, I wish
them only enough of Theban land to die in.

      You think I have no idea what is going on?
You suppose I haven't heard the oracle's words
from Apollo and Zeus himself? Your lying mouth
disgusts me, and your smarmy speechifying
makes me sick. Don't stand there like a lump
with your vile mouth hanging open. But go away.
And leave me here, contented with my life.

CREON
Whom do you suppose this kind of talk
is likely to hurt worse, yourself or me?

OEDIPUS
All I want is that you do not persuade them
any more than you have persuaded me.

CREON
Miserable man, you never had any sense
and seem still not to have got any smarter.

OEDIPUS
You are clever with your tongue, but I distrust
any man who speaks well on all subjects.

CREON
All that counts is that I am speaking rightly.

OEDIPUS
And briefly and straightforwardly, too! You?

CREON
Yes. You are the one with the devious mind.

OEDIPUS
Just go away, will you? For them and for me,
I ask you not to linger here any longer
keeping an eye on me.

CREON
                              I call on these men
and also on my people to bear witness
to the insolent answers you've given me. If I ever
get my hands on you . . .

OEDIPUS

You will do what?
What would you dare in the full view of these allies?

CREON

Whether I touch you or not, you shall suffer pain!

OEDIPUS

That's a threat I'm sure you're about to explain.

CREON

I have one of your daughters. I've sent her away.
The other one I soon shall have as well.

OEDIPUS

Omoi!

CREON

You shall have greater cause to say, "Omoi!"

OEDIPUS

You have my daughter.

CREON

Yes, and I will have
this one too.

OEDIPUS

[To the CHORUS.]

Ah, my hosts and protectors!
What will you do? Will you betray me now
or drive this villain out of Athenian lands?

FIRST CHORISTER

Leave us at once, stranger. Your present actions
as well as those in the past have not been righteous.

CREON

[To his SOLDIERS.]
If the girl will not go willingly, take her away.

ANTIGONE
Where can I run to? To what god or man
can I turn for help?

SECOND CHORISTER
                        Stop it! What are you doing?

CREON
I shall not touch this man, but only her,
who belongs, after all, to me.

OEDIPUS
                        My lords, I beseech you!

FIRST CHORISTER
Stranger, what you are doing is wrong.

CREON
                                        It's right.

FIRST CHORISTER
How can it be right?

CREON
                        I'm within my rights.
She belongs to my house.

[The SOLDIERS seize ANTIGONE's arms.]

OEDIPUS
                        I call upon the city!

FIRST CHORISTER
Stranger, I warn you. Let her go or else
it will come to a trial of strength.

CREON
                                        Stand back, I tell you.

FIRST CHORISTER
And let you do this vile thing? Certainly not!

CREON
Lay a hand on me and it will mean war
between our two cities.

OEDIPUS

[To the CHORUS.]
                              Did I not warn you before?

SECOND CHORISTER
Let go of the girl at once.

CREON
                        Don't give me orders
you haven't the strength to enforce.

SECOND CHORISTER
                                    Sir, let her go!

CREON
Bugger off!

[The SOLDIERS pull ANTIGONE toward the right.]

CHORUS
Help! Men of Colonus! Help us! Stop him!
The city is being violated! Come, help us!

ANTIGONE
Oh friends, help me. They're dragging me away!

OEDIPUS
Child? Where are you?

ANTIGONE
                              They're taking me away!

OEDIPUS
Hold out your hands to me.

ANTIGONE
I can't. They are too strong.

CREON

[To the SOLDIERS.]
                              Get it over with.

[The SOLDIERS drag ANTIGONE off, left.]

OEDIPUS
What wretchedness! What woe!

CREON
                              Never again
will these two crutches be there for you to lean on.
You want to conquer your own city, and I
have therefore done this for the people of Thebes,
obeying their command, although I am king.

Go on and win your victory, if you can.
You'll find out that once more you've done no good
letting your anger lead you on to ruin.

FIRST CHORISTER
Stay there, stranger.

CREON
                              I tell you, do not touch me.

FIRST CHORISTER
I will not let you go. You've taken the girls!

CREON
And if you don't unhand me, those two won't be
the only captives I'll take.

FIRST CHORISTER
                              What do you mean?

CREON

[Indicating OEDIPUS.]
I'll take him, too.

FIRST CHORISTER
                              That's outrageous!

CREON
                                          Is it?
I don't see your king anywhere about.
Will he pop out of the bushes to try to stop me?

OEDIPUS
Is it just loud talk, or will you indeed
lay hands on me?

CREON
                              Just shut your mouth, old man!

OEDIPUS
No! The goddesses here can no longer restrain me
from uttering the curse that is on my lips.
You are a villain, vicious, violent, and vile,
and have taken from me the eyes that I still had
after I lost my own. Therefore I pray
the all-seeing Sun may beat down upon your head
and house and grant you an old age as painful as mine!

CREON
Men of this land, you hear how he goes on?

OEDIPUS
They see us both, and they can tell that I
am the victim of actions but you merely of words.

CREON
My anger is beyond control. Old
as I am, and slow, and alone, I shall still carry
this man away by force.

OEDIPUS
                              Woe! Woe!

SECOND CHORISTER
This is insolence, stranger. You cannot do this!

CREON
Watch me!

FIRST CHORISTER
                    If you could, what kind of city
would Athens be?

CREON
                    With justice on his side
a little man can vanquish someone greater.

OEDIPUS
You hear what he is saying?

THIRD CHORISTER
                    He won't do it,
I swear, as Zeus is my witness.

CREON
                    What Zeus thinks
he knows, but surely you don't.

FIRST CHORISTER
                              This is disgraceful.

CREON
And what do you propose to do about it?

FIRST CHORISTER
I call on the lords of this land and on the people!

THIRD CHORISTER
Come, help us. These strangers go too far.

[THESEUS enters, followed by his SOLDIERS.]

THESEUS
Who is crying for help? What is this ruckus?
I was sacrificing to the god Poseidon,
the patron of Colonus, and here is this clamor
interrupting the rite. What's going on
to hurry me here this way?

OEDIPUS
                                    My dear, dear friend,
it's wonderful to hear your voice. I've suffered
terrible treatment from this most terrible man.

THESEUS
From whom? What pain? Tell me what is the trouble.

OEDIPUS
It's Creon. He has taken both my daughters.

THESEUS
What? What are you telling me?

OEDIPUS
                                    Just that.

THESEUS
One of you hurry back to the altar and tell them,
all of them, to hurry on foot and on horseback
and head them off at the pass where the two roads join.
They should be able to get there first. If not,
this stranger will have made me look like a fool!
[Turning to CREON.]
As for him, I am angry enough to want to kill him,
but I shall let the law run its normal course.
You shall never leave this country until you've returned

those girls you've taken. I want to see them here
alive and well. Your actions are a disgrace
to me, and of course to you. You should be ashamed
of yourself and your country! You come to a place like Athens
that respects the laws and justice and you behave
like a band of brigands! Did you think that we were slaves?
Weak? Stupid? Did you think I count for nothing?
      But then, it isn't Thebes that made you evil.
Thebes doesn't breed wicked men. And Thebes
would not praise what you've done here, invading us
and plundering, kidnapping suppliants. You
have done, all on your own, what I could never
imagine doing—entering a country
without the consent of the ruler, whoever he was,
and dragging people off. I would have known
how strangers are supposed to behave themselves.
You have brought shame to your city, which does not deserve it.
Age brings wisdom to some but not to you.
In your advancing years, you are turning senile.
      I say again, and you had better believe me,
that those girls must be brought here, otherwise—
mark my words—you shall be my captive.

SECOND CHORISTER
We tried to warn you, stranger. Look where you are.
Whoever you are, this is what wickedness gets you.

CREON
I did not mean to imply, son of Aegeus,
that Athens has no men. Absolutely not.
And my action was less rash than it might appear,
for I could not imagine that your city would want

to keep my relatives here against my will.
Whom are we talking about? A parricide!
A man of great impurity whose children
are the fruit of an unholy, unspeakable marriage.
I know the laws of Athens and I admire
the wisdom of the council that meets on Ares'
hill—and in this knowledge I put my trust,
believing that such exiles could not be welcome.
Even so, I would not have presumed to touch him
had he not called down curses on my head
and on my family, too. That affront required
an answer. There is no old age for anger;
it's only the dead who are immune from insults.
You will do as you will. Alone and weak, I cannot
stop you now, but old as I am, one day
I shall contrive somehow to answer you back.

OEDIPUS
Insolent, shameless liar! Are these outrageous
distortions of the truth insults to my
defenseless old age or your senility?
You go on with that palaver about killings,
marriages, and other old disasters—
in all of which I was the unwitting
victim of angry gods. But nothing you say
touches my character, which is all a man
controls. For the terrible things I did to myself
and my kin I cannot be blamed. A prophecy came
from the oracle to my father that he would die
at his child's hand. Am I to be reproached
for that? I wasn't there; I hadn't been
conceived or born. I came into the world

and if I came to blows one day with a stranger
I had no idea who he was or what I was doing.
And are you not ashamed of yourself, you maggot,
for making me speak of my marriage to your sister,
who turned out to be my mother—although I had no
hint of that? But you have no sense of decent
limits. Yes, she bore me, alas, and then
she bore me children, and I am ashamed, ashamed,
but that was nothing I had willed, as you know,
and your abuse of her and of me is nasty,
hypocritical, calculated garbage.
Nothing that you have said about the murder
or the marriage demonstrates that I am evil.
Answer me one question. If somebody here
threatened to kill you, would your first thought be
to ask if he might be your father? Or would
you fight, strike back at him, and protect yourself?
You want to save your life, and do not think
of the possible complications, which can wait.
That was the sorry situation the gods
had contrived for me. If my father's ghost came back
he would not contradict what I'm saying here.
But you, a villain, a wicked opportunist,
assert whatever you please, true, half-true,
not true at all, just so long as it works
to reproach me and defame me in these men's eyes.
You flatter Theseus, fawn on him and Athens,
but you ought to know that what you say is truer
than you suppose, for Athens honors the gods
in a way you would not begin to understand.
Athens respects the divine laws that safeguard

suppliants like me. You come to snatch me
from their protection, a weak, defenseless old man,
and have already carried off my dear daughters.
And on account of this I call on these
goddesses in supplication and pray
for their protection and help, so that you may learn
what kind of city this is and what kind of men
live here and guard it, and make it what it is.

SECOND CHORISTER
My lord, the stranger is persuasive, a good
man, unfortunate, but still our guest.

THESEUS
Enough talking. His soldiers are getting away,
and we are just standing here.

CREON

                                    And what decision
have you made for me, an utterly helpless man?

THESEUS
You will lead me to the children. If you have them
hidden away, you'll show me. If your men
are fleeing toward Thebes, then mine will intercept them
along the way so that they will never thank
the gods that they got away safely. Now let's go.
The captor is now the captive; the hunter is now
the quarry. What wickedness and cunning gain
they do not keep for long. You understand
my meaning, or do I simply waste my breath?

CREON
To what you say here, I cannot object,
but later, when I'm at home, then we shall see . . .

THESEUS
If you must threaten me, do it on the way.
Oedipus, you stay here, and be assured
that I shall find your children and bring them back
safe and in your arms or die trying.

OEDIPUS
My blessings, Theseus, and my thanks for your noble
and righteous actions. And, of course, I wish you luck.

[THESEUS and CREON exit right, followed by SOLDIERS.]

Ode III

FIRST CHORISTER
Oh, to be there, to hear
the din of battle, to see
the wheeling and rearing horses
on the strand in the clear light
of afternoon or at Daphnae's seaside
near Apollo's temple,
or else perhaps at Eleusis
where we could make them out
by the torchlight of the silent priests
of Persephone and Demeter.
There might Theseus make his stand
to retrieve the captives, the virgin sisters.

SECOND CHORISTER

Or are they coming together
to the west of the white rock
of Mount Aigaleos in Oea's deme,
on swift horses and bright rattling chariots?
Powerful is the rush of Ares, and bright
are the spearpoints of Theseus' sons.
On both sides bridles flash
and men ride with loose reins,
but our Athena is mistress of horses
and for Rhea's son, Poseidon, our protector,
our steeds will outdo themselves.

THIRD CHORISTER

Do they delay? Or are they fighting now?
My mind tells me the girls, who have suffered so,
mistreated by their own kindred, will suffer
no more. This day will the great Zeus
bring his obscure purpose at last to fruition.
I can foresee our triumph in this encounter.
I only wish I could fly like some great bird
to gaze from the heights of the clouds at the contest below.

FIRST CHORISTER

All-seeing Zeus, supreme among the gods,
grant our guardians absolute success
in their righteous strife to seize their prey.
I call upon you and your reverend daughter Athena,
I call upon hunter Apollo and on Diana,
who follows the quick deer on the hillside,
to give aid to our men, this land, and us.

Scene IV

THIRD CHORISTER
Honored guest, you will have no complaint
that your host's promise was left unkept. I see
those daughters of yours coming this way with their guards.

OEDIPUS
What? What are you saying? Where?

ANTIGONE
                                                    O father,
if only the gods could grant you vision to see
this noble man who has brought us back to you.

OEDIPUS
Child! Both of you? Safe?

ANTIGONE
                                        Both of us! Safe!
Theseus and his soldiers rescued us.

OEDIPUS
Come, let me hug you close. I hardly hoped
you'd ever return to me so that I could hold you.

ANTIGONE
That hug you want is what we both have longed for.

OEDIPUS
Where are you? Come to me?

ANTIGONE
                                        Yes, yes, we are coming.

OEDIPUS
My dear children!

ANTIGONE
                          To a parent, all children are dear.

OEDIPUS
Crutches that support a frail old man.

ANTIGONE
Sad crutches, of a very sad man . . .

OEDIPUS
No, not so sad. Not now. I have what I hold
most dear in the world. And were I to die now
with you two here beside me, how bad would that be?
Hold me tight, as if we could grow together
and know what comfort I take from your support
in all our wanderings. Now, tell me what happened.

ANTIGONE
He was our savior, father. His was the deed.
Let him tell it, as he deserves to do.

OEDIPUS
My host and protector, I do beg your forgiveness.
My joy in seeing my children again, for whom
I had given up all hope, was so great that it made me
neglect my manners. But I ask your understanding.
You, after all, are the cause of this distracting
happiness I feel. And you must know
that I wish that the gods may grant you and your country
all that you desire. Among the many
men I have met, you have distinguished yourself

in piety, truth, and justice. For your good deeds
I have only inadequate words with which to repay you.
But stretch our your hand to me that I may touch it,
or let me kiss your cheek in thanks and love . . .
        But what am I saying? I am tainted with evil
and was born to misfortune and anguish. So unclean
a person ought not to approach someone like you.
We sufferers ought to huddle discreetly together
sharing our misery. From where you stand, receive
my greetings, thanks, and good wishes. And I beg you,
continue as you have begun and offer me still
the protection your great piety has prompted.

THESEUS
That you have talked with your daughters first is only
natural. Your delight in your reunion
causes me no pain at all. I prefer
to live through deeds rather than mere words,
and in your love for them you have displayed
your gratitude. My inclination toward action
you have learned, for I've failed to keep no promise
I made to you, and here I stand, old sir,
presenting them to you, alive, unhurt,
after the dire threats that were made against them.
As to how we won the fight, I dislike boasting,
and you will surely hear from them what happened.
        But let me change the subject and ask your views.
As I was on my way here, something came up
that surprised me and that you should know about.

OEDIPUS
What is it, son of Aegeus. I've no idea
what you could be talking of. What surprise?

THESEUS
They tell me there is a man—not from Thebes,
but one who says he is related to you.
He is sitting now at the base of Poseidon's altar
where I had been sacrificing when I set forth,
and he asks for sanctuary.

OEDIPUS
                    Where is he from?
And from what is he asking sanctuary here?

THESEUS
All I know is that he has asked for a brief
word with you.

OEDIPUS
              With me? What's it about?
To sit in supplication is no small thing.

THESEUS
He wants to speak with you and then leave in safety.

OEDIPUS
I cannot imagine. You don't know who this is?

THESEUS
Do you know anyone in Argos who'd ask you a favor?

OEDIPUS
Argos? Dear friend, don't say another word.

THESEUS
But what is the matter?

OEDIPUS

        No more. Let us drop it.

THESEUS

Drop what?

OEDIPUS

        When you said "Argos," I knew who it was.

THESEUS

And who is this person whom I must now dislike?

OEDIPUS

My lord, it is a son of mine. Whom I hate.
No voice could cause me greater pain than his.

THESEUS

Could you not listen to what he asks and then
simply refuse? Why is it painful to hear him?

OEDIPUS

This man's voice is detestable. His father
cannot bear it. Indulge me in this, please.

THESEUS

But he is a suppliant! Does that not oblige you?
Ought you not to maintain respect for the gods?

ANTIGONE

Father, I am young to be giving advice,
but let me try to persuade you. Let this pious
man give the god his wish and yield to us.
Let our brother approach. Nothing he says

can make you swerve in your judgment. And what harm
can come from simply listening to his words?
There could even be some advantage, for evil actions
sometimes reveal themselves in speech beforehand.
And remember, you are his father. Even if he
had committed terrible crimes against you, it still
would be wrong to return evil for his evil.
Show him mercy. Other fathers have had
wicked children with terrible tempers and still
allowed themselves to be mollified by their friends.
Do not think of the present, but of the past
and the sufferings you endured because of your parents.
Evil is everywhere and it stays alive
from the justifiable grudges we hold onto.
Though robbed of your sight, your intellect is keen.
Yield to us. It is not right that those
who wish you well should be obliged to beg you.
For the kindnesses you have received, you should grant
a kindness.

OEDIPUS
                    To such sweet words, how can I answer
no? Let it be as you have said. But my lord,
promise, if this man comes, to protect my life.

THESEUS
I do not need to hear your request a second
time. I do not boast but have already shown
that as long as I live, your life, too, shall be safe.

[Exit THESEUS]

Ode IV

FIRST CHORISTER
Whoever is greedy for more in life
than a moderate portion
of goods and pleasures
is wrong, and cannot see
how, as the days spin out
pain from their long skein,
the end is the same for all
at the gate of Hades.
There, you bring nothing with you,
not even the recollection of wedding songs,
no lyre, no dance
in that unmoving silence.

SECOND CHORISTER
Never to have been born is best.
Everyone knows that, and a close second,
once you have appeared in this life, is a quick
return, as soon as you can, to where you came from.
In our light-headed youth we carry
blithe ideas, not knowing what blows await,
what hardships are bearing down, closer and closer.
Murder, hatred, strife, resentment, and envy
are lurking, and then, behind them, bitter old age,
powerless, friendless, with evils our only neighbors.

THIRD CHORISTER
Look at this unfortunate man here,
battered on all sides, like a cape facing north
so that winter winds and tides assault and the grim
waves tear at him every which way, and ruin

breaks over his head again and again,
some from the west where the sun goes down,
more from the east where the new day dawns,
and then, from the south, where a wan sun shines at noon,
more torment yet. At midnight, from mountains behind
there is nothing else. The geography is pain,
and nowhere can you find pleasure or respite.

Scene V

ANTIGONE
Here is the suppliant, father. He comes alone,
without companions or guards. And he is weeping.

OEDIPUS
And who is this?

ANTIGONE
                        It is Polyneices, father.

[Enter POLYNEICES.]

POLYNEICES
Omoi! What can I do? Shall I weep for myself
or for my aged father's manifest sorrows,
here in a foreign land, dressed like a beggar,
the alien dirt all over his withered flesh,
his sightless eyes, and his uncombed hair the breezes
tousle so roughly? It breaks my heart to see him,
poor, hungry, and suffering! I am a wicked
son, the worst of men, to have come so late
to see him and to have done so little to help.

No other men need accuse me, for I proclaim
my guilt, myself. And I pray to divine Mercy
who shares the throne of Zeus to be the protector
that I ought to have been. My crimes can be
atoned for—surely they cannot be any worse.

[A pause.]
No answer, father? You turn away in silence?
Will you send me away in utter humiliation
without even a word of reproach? Sisters,
can you not help me? Can you not move him to soften
his heart enough at least to make some reply?
Shall he send me away in disgrace, a suppliant son
protected by the god, without any answer?

ANTIGONE
Speak to him yourself, brother. Your words
bringing delight or pity or even anger
may prompt a word from one who has been speechless.

POLYNEICES
Well, I shall speak to him then. Your advice seems good,
and perhaps I shall have Poseidon's help from whose
altar this land's ruler raised me up
and gave me the right to speak and then leave in peace.
As I expect to receive these things from the strangers
who are here with us, I also look to you,
my sisters and my father, with that same hope.

But let me get to the point, father, and tell you
how I have been driven from Thebes and into exile,
because I claimed, as the firstborn, that I had the right
to sit on the throne and exercise royal power.
For this, my younger brother, Eteocles,

banished me. He did not accomplish this
by any debate or even by force of arms,
but somehow persuaded the city to his side.
I cannot say how this happened except that the Furies
that pursue you were also hounding me.
This is what seers I consulted said had happened.

   I went to Argos and there I was married. Adrastus,
who became my father-in-law, found allies for me,
fighters of the Peloponnese who could join
in an expedition of seven troops of spearmen
to assert my lawful claim and either die
or reclaim for me the throne of Thebes, and exile
those usurpers who had exiled me.

   So, why have I come here, father? To ask your aid
for me and my allies who now surround
the land of Thebes. These are such men as the great
spear-wielding Amphiarius, brave and gifted
in reading the signs of the birds that fly overhead.
Tydeus, too, is there, from Aetolia, Oeneus'
son; and Eteoclus, the native of Argos.
The fourth is Hippomedon, whose father, Talaus,
sent him. The fifth is Capaneus, who boasts
that he will destroy Thebes and burn it down.
Parthenopaeus is sixth, Atalanta's son.
And I, who am your son and not your son,
but, say, the son of an evil destiny, lead
this band of fighters of Argos against Thebes.

   All of us beseech you, in supplication,
in the name of my sisters, and for your own soul's sake,
to relent in your anger toward me as I go forth
to punish my brother who robbed me of my throne
and country, too. The oracles have said—

if we can believe them—that whichever side you favor
will, in this struggle, prevail. Think of our sacred
fountains, and think of our people's gods, and be
persuaded in this to take my side. We both
are beggars, exiles, living on the dole
and the kindnesses of others. We share our fate,
and that tyrant in Thebes luxuriates and laughs
at us both. Stand by me, and I shall destroy him,
drive him out, set you up again
in your own house, and take the throne for myself.
If you and I are together in this, we can do it.
Otherwise, the prospects for success
or even, for that matter, survival are dim.

FIRST CHORISTER
For Theseus' sake, who sent him here, say something.
Give him some answer before you turn him away.

OEDIPUS
Guardians of this land, if it had not been
Theseus who sent him here, believing
that it was right for me to speak to him,
he would not have heard my voice. But he shall depart
having enjoyed this favor, although it shall not
please him.

[To POLYNEICES]

                Wretch! When you were holding the scepter
your brother now holds in Thebes, you sent me away,
drove your own father into exile,
cityless, dressed in rags as you see me here,
so that my appearance makes you weep,
because only now do you understand what it's like,

sharing my troubles. But I am not weeping! I
have learned to bear what I must, and it is anger
that fills my heart, remembering what you did,
the murderer of my life, for it was you
who put me on this regimen of begging,
this diet of grief, disgrace, and other men's crumbs.
If I didn't have these daughters to rely on,
I could not have survived. From what you did,
I would have died. But they have kept me alive,
my nurses, my aids. They are not women but men
whose strength has preserved me. But my sons are not sons,
or surely you two are no sons of mine.

      And this is how the gods above look down
and see you for the villain that you are.
And if your squadrons march toward Thebes they shall watch
and delight in your failure, for certainly you shall fail,
polluted by bloodshed, both you and your brother.
Such are the curses I called down on your head
many times in the past, and now you can hear me
as I pronounce them once again. Let curses
attend you both as you fight with one another
and teach you some respect for your begetters.
I may be blind, but I can see that your sisters
behaved better, were loyal and decent. But you?
For your supplication, my curses. The only throne
you will ever get near will be that of mighty Zeus
beside which Justice sits. He will pass sentence
upon you for your breaking of ancient laws.

      Be off. I spit on you. I am no longer
your father, wretch of wretches, villain of villains.
All you get from me is curses. May you
never rule the land of your kinfolk and never

return to low-lying Argos. You will die by
your brother's hand, and you will kill him.
I call on Tartaros' darkness to give you the only
home you deserve, and on these goddesses here,
and on the god of war, who put this hatred
into your minds, to give you what you deserve.
Now, you have heard my voice and have my answer.
Go away, and tell your trusty allies
and the Thebans, too, that this is Oedipus' wish,
the legacy he has bestowed upon his sons.

FIRST CHORISTER
Polyneices, your arrival here
has not been a joy, but your departure will be.
Go, at once.

POLYNEICES
                    I, too, regret my coming.
I am sorry for myself and my companions.
What an end to our long march from Argos!
I cannot even tell them what was said here,
nor turn back from the battle, but I must meet
my fate in lonely silence.
                    Sisters, you've heard
our father pronounce his terrible curse. But I ask you,
if what he predicts comes true, and somehow you
are back in Thebes, do not dishonor me,
but place me in my tomb with the proper rites.
To the praise you have earned already for your service
to your afflicted father, more shall be added
for what you shall have done for your woeful brother.

ANTIGONE
Polyneices, I beg you, listen to me,
and be persuaded by my advice!

POLYNEICES
                              What?
Dearest Antigone, what do you want to tell me?

ANTIGONE
Turn back your army to Argos. Do not destroy
yourself and the city.

POLYNEICES
                    I cannot do it. How
could I bring the army back with me? How can I give
orders if I am a coward before my friends?

ANTIGONE
Do not be angry, brother. Only think!
What good will it do you to ruin Thebes?

POLYNEICES
To run is shameful. I am the elder brother.
He is the younger, and mocks me. It isn't right!

ANTIGONE
Have you not heard the prophecies of this man?
He says you will die at one another's hands.

POLYNEICES.
That's what he wants. We can give it to him.

ANTIGONE
Poor desperate man! But who will follow you,
knowing that such an outcome is foretold?

POLYNEICES
No one will know. A good commander's duty
is to tell the troops good news and hold back bad.

ANTIGONE
Then your mind is made up? There's nothing I can say?

POLYNEICES
It is. And do not delay me. My duty is clear,
to see to this hard march, ill-fated, even
evil, as my father says, and the Fates.
But you may please Zeus if you do me that favor
I asked of you.

[They embrace.]
                              Now, let me go. Farewell.
Never again shall you see me in this life.

ANTIGONE
Oh, miserable!

POLYNEICES
                              Do not lament for me.

ANTIGONE
Who would not weep for you, brother? Who could
watch, dry-eyed, as you set out for your death?

POLYNEICES
If I must die, I must.

ANTIGONE

But you do not have to!
Only do as I've asked!

POLYNEICES

Do not attempt
to change my mind. There's nothing you can say.

ANTIGONE
Then, woe upon woe, if I am to lose you, brother.

POLYNEICES
These things are fated. We have less choice than we think.
But I pray to the gods that you may not suffer evil.
The gods in heaven know that you don't deserve it.

[Exit POLYNEICES.]

Ode V

FIRST CHORISTER
New evils from a new direction,
with a hard fate the blind stranger
delivers to his son.
Who can say that the gods' purpose
will not be fulfilled?

[There is a sound of thunder.]

SECOND CHORISTER
Time looks on,
looks on at everything,
tearing down one day

and raising up another.
The sky sounds forth. O Zeus!

[Again, thunder.]

OEDIPUS
Children, children, if someone is there could he bring
Theseus here, the best of men?

ANTIGONE
                                        Father,
why do you want him summoned here?

OEDIPUS
                                        That thunder,
the winged thunder of Zeus. It will carry me soon
to Hades. Bring him here, and do it quickly.

[Again, thunder.]

FIRST CHORISTER
Another crash, unspeakable,
sent by Zeus. It resounds,
spreads terror to make the hairs on my head prickle.
My spirit shrinks at the lightning
that blazes across the sky.

SECOND CHORISTER
What can this mean?
Will the god cast his thunderbolt?
I am fearful. It never shoots down
for no reason. And it never bodes well.

[Again, thunder.]
We look up at a vast sky! O Zeus!

OEDIPUS
Children, the end of life that has been foretold
has come upon me. There's no way to put it off.

ANTIGONE
How do you know this? What makes you think so?

OEDIPUS

I know.

Have someone go as quickly as he can.
Bring the ruler of this land to me.

[Again, thunder.]

THIRD CHORISTER
Ahh! Ahh! Again.
Another peal that echoes around us.
Oh, may the gods be kind and bring us
something good wrapped in this darkness,
down to our mother earth!

[Again, thunder.]

SECOND CHORISTER
May we find that you are in a favorable mood,
and may this encounter we have had with a man
accursed not taint us, too, with another curse.
Oh, Zeus! We implore you!

OEDIPUS
Is he here yet? Will he find me still alive
and alert, my children?

ANTIGONE
                                  Father, why
do you worry about the state of your mind?

OEDIPUS
                                        He was kind,
and in return for his kindness, I wish to make
that payment I promised when he took us in.

FIRST CHORISTER
Oh, oh! Come, come my son.
Leave those clefts in the high rocks where you perform
the sacrifice of oxen for Poseidon,
and come to us now.

SECOND CHORISTER
The stranger who made demands
of you and the city
wishes to reciprocate
good for good.
Hurry, lord, hurry.

[Again, thunder, and THESEUS enters from the left.]

Scene VI

THESEUS
What is this with all of you making a fuss,
and our guest as well? You think the sky is falling?

It could be a sign from Zeus, or it could just be
a sudden squall. Who knows, when such weather happens?

OEDIPUS
Lord, your appearance here is welcome indeed.
And one of the gods has blessed you in your coming.

THESEUS
Son of Laius, what do you mean?

OEDIPUS
                                    My life
is drawing to a close. The balance shifts.
And I do not want to die without fulfilling
the promises I have made to you and your city.

THESEUS
What makes you think that your death is so near?

OEDIPUS
                                            The signal
comes from the gods, who herald it to me
with the signs they have been making.

THESEUS
                                        You think it is clear
and unmistakable, old man?

OEDIPUS
                                All that thunder
and all those bolts of lightning that come from Zeus'
unconquerable hand.

THESEUS

           I am convinced.

Your prophecies before have never proven

false. Tell me, what do you want me to do?

OEDIPUS

I will tell you, son of Aegeus, what things

are destined for your city by the powers

that age cannot destroy. I will show you

without any guiding hand to assist me, the place

where I must die. You must never reveal

to any human being where it is hidden

or where to try to find it. But understand

that its proximity gives Athens protection,

stronger than many shields or spears from some allied

army. These things are mysteries, not to be

explained, but you shall learn them when you go there

alone—always alone, for I do not tell

these townsmen or even my own children, although

I love them. You must always keep this secret,

and when you come to the end of your life, tell only

your chosen heir, and let him only tell his.

If you do this, your city shall never be

ravaged by those who sprang from the dragon's teeth.

Any number of cities, however well

governed, can allow themselves to decline.

The gods see these things clearly but can be slow

to make correction, when men forget religion

and turn to extremes of madness. Son of Aegeus,

I know you would never wish that upon Athens.

        That much you know already. Let us go now

to the sacred place, for the power of the god

is present. I can feel it hurry me on.
Let us dawdle no longer. Daughters, follow,
and let me guide you as you have guided me.
Do not touch me, but let me find my way
to the sacred tomb where it is fated for me
to be hidden in this earth. This way. This way.
For I am now led by Hermes and the infernal
goddess. O dark light, you once were mine
but my body feels you now for the last time
as I set off for Hades to hide the end
of my existence. Come, dearest of strangers,
farewell, and may you always have good fortune,
you, your attendants, and all this land. Remember
me and my death in your prosperity
forever as you enjoy your great success.

[Exit OEDIPUS, ANTIGONE, ISMENE, and THESEUS,
to the right.]

Ode VI

FIRST CHORISTER
O Dark Lady the living never
see, who frightens us who are alive,
and you, Dark Lord of those who dwell
in the night that is forever,
hear our prayer: we wish the stranger well
and ask that he may arrive
without pain
on the vast plain
that holds all those below
where the waters of Styx flow,

and after the many troubles he has seen
may a just god exalt him and wash him clean.

SECOND CHORISTER
And you who appear as a beast in Hades' lair,
the growling guardian there,
as our ancient legends say,
where strangers pass by but only one way,
may he have a gentle passage, free of danger,
O child of Earth and Tartaros, bless this stranger,
who comes to the dark plain of the dead. Keep
him well, I pray you, who are eternal sleep.

Scene VII

[Enter MESSENGER.]

MESSENGER
Men of the city, the short version is
that Oedipus is dead. But those few words
do not begin to convey what happened there.

FIRST CHORISTER
The poor man is dead then?

MESSENGER
                                        Oh, yes.
No question. He has left our mundane life.

SECOND CHORISTER
How did it happen? Was it blessedly painless?

MESSENGER

It was something to wonder at. How he left here
you know perfectly well. You saw it yourselves.
With none of his friends to guide him, he himself
directed us all. But when he came to the threshold
that leads down into the earth with brazen steps,
he stopped at one of the many diverging paths
near that hollow basin dedicated
to Pirithous' and Theseus' bond of friendship.
Between this and the Thorician rock he stopped
and sat down by the hollow pear tree there
and at the marble tomb and took off his filthy
rags. He called on his daughters to bring him fresh
running water to wash in and to pour as libation.
They went to Demeter's green hill and fetched
the water, bathed their father, and helped him dress
in the customary garments. When this was done,
Zeus of the earth thundered yet again,
and the girls shuddered in terror when they heard it,
fell to clasp their father's knees, and wept,
beating their breasts and wailing, and when he heard them
he folded them in his arms and said, "My children,
on this day your father is no more. It's over.
No more shall you have the tiresome task of tending
a blind old man. It was hard, but all these hardships
dissolve at the single statement I make to you here—
that no one has loved you more than I. And now
you two will spend the rest of your lives without me."
    They huddled together that way, sobbing, and then
when their lamenting was done and they fell silent,
there was a voice that called out from one place and another,
hailing him, and the hairs on our heads stood upright

in awe, for we knew the voice was that of a god:
"You, Oedipus, why do you tarry? Come,
you have delayed too long." And Oedipus knew
it was the god calling him, and he told our Lord
Theseus to approach him. When he came near,
Oedipus said, "My dear friend, give your hand
in a pledge of friendship to my children here,
and you, daughters, give your hands to him,
and promise, Theseus, that you will never betray them,
that you will look after them always, and be kind."

      Noble Theseus gave his oath, not
out of pity, that he would do this for his guest.
And then, Oedipus laid his groping hands
upon his children's heads and said to them,
"Daughters, you must be brave. Now, walk away
and do not look on what you should not see,
or listen to what you should not hear, but go,
without delay. Leave me with Theseus here,
who is in charge and alone may witness this."

      We all heard this, and then we went with the girls,
all of us weeping, and after we had left
we looked back and saw that he was no longer there.
Theseus held his hands in front of his face
as if to shade his eyes or hide them from
some terrifying sight he could not bear.
But then we saw him salute the earth and the sky,
the home of the gods. But how Oedipus died
no mortal except for Theseus can report.
There was no thunderbolt from the sky, no whirlwind
rising up from the sea. But some escort
came in kindness from the gods of the sky
or from under the earth to lead him on his way.

There were no lamentations, no suffering from disease,
but what we mortals call miraculous.
If anyone here thinks this is foolishness,
very well then, he may call me a fool.

SECOND CHORISTER
And where are the girls and their escorts?

MESSENGER

                                They approach.
The sounds of their weeping are coming closer.

[Enter ANTIGONE and ISMENE.]

Ode VII

ANTIGONE
Aieee! It is for us to make lamentation
for the cursed blood of our father that is in us,
an unhappy pair who endured, for our father's sake,
endless pain. And we shall always bear
the griefs that tormented him beyond all reason,
that we have witnessed and therefore suffered too.

FIRST CHORISTER
What has happened?

ANTIGONE
                We can only guess.

SECOND CHORISTER
He is gone?

ANTIGONE
                    It was a good end. Not war
and not the turbulent sea took him from us,
but to the vast dark plain he was carried off
in an ending that was a mystery. The darkness
you and I face, poor sister, is staying alive
without him, as we wander together over
distant lands or the billows of restless seas.

ISMENE
How can we bear it? May deadly Hades take me
so that I share my aged father's death.
The life that I have left is not worth living.

FIRST CHORISTER
O excellent daughters, you must be brave and accept
what the gods have sent. Avoid excessive passion.
No one can find fault with the path you have trodden.

ANTIGONE
One may even grieve for the loss of grief, or for things
that were never dear when he was alive and I held him
in my arms. O father, o dear father! Now
you are clothed in the earth's darkness. But even there
you have my love and hers.

SECOND CHORISTER
                    He lived . . .

ANTIGONE
                                        He lived
just as he chose.

THIRD CHORISTER
                    How do you mean?

ANTIGONE
                         He died
where he wanted, here in a foreign land. And he lies
on his shady bed forever, beyond all mourning.
These eyes of mine are weeping for him in a pain
I do not know how I can bear—that he died
without me.

ISMENE
                    Poor sister! What fate awaits us,
alone as we are?

FIRST CHORISTER
                         Dear friends, remember his end
was happy, blessed. Leave off your grieving. Think
that none of us is secure against misfortune.

ANTIGONE
Sister, let us go back there.

ISMENE
                         Why?

ANTIGONE
                                        I have
a sudden longing . . .

ISMENE
                    For what?

ANTIGONE

                               To see his home

underneath the earth.

ISMENE

                  Whose home?

ANTIGONE

                           Our father's.

ISMENE

But it is forbidden!

ANTIGONE

                Sister, do not rebuke me.

ISMENE

And besides . . .

ANTIGONE

                What? What is it?

ISMENE

                           He has no tomb.

He died alone. There is nothing to see.

ANTIGONE

                           Even so,

Take me there, and then kill me.

ISMENE

                    {And stay behind?}

ANTIGONE

{I suppose we could kill each other.}[2]

ISMENE

Wretched, wretched.
What future do we have? How do we trudge,
bereft and helpless, through a dreary life?

FIRST CHORISTER
My friends, take courage.

ANTIGONE

Where shall we take refuge?

SECOND CHORISTER
You have found one . . .

ANTIGONE

What?

SECOND CHORISTER

. . . where you'll be safe.

ANTIGONE
I think . . .

FIRST CHORISTER
What?

ANTIGONE

How can we go home?

FIRST CHORISTER
Don't even try.

ANTIGONE

I hear there's trouble there.

SECOND CHORISTER
There was trouble there before.

ANTIGONE
There was nothing we could do then. Now, things are worse.

THIRD CHORISTER
Your life appears to have been unremitting trouble.

ANTIGONE
Yes, yes, it has.

SECOND CHORISTER
                                    Dreadful, dreadful.

ANTIGONE
Ohhh! Ohhh! Where do we go, O Zeus?
To what extremity now does the god drive us?

Exodos

[Enter THESEUS.]

THESEUS
Girls, stop your weeping. One should not mourn
for those for whom the darkness is a treasure,
a gift from the gods. The gods might take offense.

ANTIGONE
Son of Aegeus, the two of us beg you . . .

THESEUS
What is the request you make of me?

ANTIGONE
We wish to see for ourselves our father's tomb.

THESEUS
But it is not permitted that you should do this.

ANTIGONE
Lord of Athens, what do you mean? Why?

THESEUS
Girls, he instructed me never to go there myself,
and never to tell any mortal of the sacred
place that holds him. He said that if I complied,
I would keep my country free from pain forever.
The god of oaths heard me make this promise,
the son of Zeus who harkens to all such words.

ANTIGONE
If that is what he said, then that is enough.
But send us then to Thebes, that we may attempt
to prevent the slaughter there that awaits our brothers.

THESEUS
That I will do, and anything in my power
that may be helpful, and that the one below
may approve of, who just departed. I must not fail him.

FIRST CHORISTER
Now let the lamentations cease. No more
weeping. Accept that this is how things must be.

Glossary of Names

Abae: a town in the province of Phocis in northern Greece where there was an oracle and a temple of Apollo.

Acheron: one of the rivers of Hades. Charon ferried the souls of the dead across this river.

Adrastus: a king of Argos and Polyneices' father-in-law.

Aegeus: a legendary king of Athens, father of Theseus.

Aetolia: a district in central Greece, south of Thessaly.

Agenor: a king of Tyros and a son of Poseidon. He is the father of Europa and Cadmus.

Aigaleos: a mountain in Oea.

Amphiarius: one of the seven captains supporting Polyneices in the expedition against Thebes. He was reluctant to go and hid but was betrayed by his wife Eriphyle, the sister of Adrastus.

Amphion: son of Zeus by Antiope. He and his brother Zethus built the walls of Athens.

Amphitrite: daughter of Oceanus and Tethys, whose union with Poseidon produced Triton.

Antigone: a daughter of Oedipus and Jocasta.

Aphrodite: goddess of love.

Apollo: son of Zeus and Latona, also called Phoebus. He is, among other things, the god of prophecy.

Ares: son of Zeus and Hera, and the god of war.

Argos: the capital of Argolis, a province in the Peloponnese.

Artemis: sister of Apollo and goddess of the hunt. She is also the patroness of virgins.

Atalanta: an Arcadian princess, the mother of Parthenopaeus, q.v.

Athena: daughter of Zeus, goddess of wisdom and of the arts, and patroness of Athens.

Athens: city founded by Cadmus, and the home of Sophocles.

Bacchantes: also known as the Maenads, priestesses of Dionysos who took part in frenzied rites celebrating that god.

Bacchus: also called Dionysos, the son of Zeus and Semele, the god of wine, mystery, enthusiasm, and raw poetry.

Boeotia: a territory northwest of Attica, the capital of which was Thebes.

Boreas: god of the north wind.

Cadmus: the legendary founder of Thebes. He married Harmonia, daughter of Aphrodite.

Capanaeus: one of the seven against Thebes, and the first to die in his assault on the wall.

Castalia: a spring sacred to the Muses on Mount Parnassus.

Cithaeron: a mountain ridge in southern Boeotia separating it from Attica.

Colonus: a deme, or subordinate town, of Thebes in Attica.

Corinth: a Greek city-state on the Isthmus of Corinth, which separates the Peloponnese from the mainland. It is about forty-eight miles southwest of Athens.

Creon: son of Menoeceus, brother of Jocasta, and father of Haimon. He succeeded Oedipus to the throne of Thebes.

Cronos: son of Uranos (heaven) and Gea (earth) and youngest of the Titans. He was father of Zeus.

Cyllene: the highest mountain in the Peloponnese.

Danaë: daughter of Acrisios who was told that her son would murder him. He locked her in a tower, where she was seduced by Zeus in the form of a golden rain. She bore Perseus, who years later killed Acrisios accidentally with a discus.

Daphnae: a fortress on the Syrian border near Egypt, now called Defenneh.

Daulis: a city in Phocis a few miles east of Delphi.

Delos: an island in the Aegean, the birthplace of Artemis and Apollo.

Delphi: a city in Phocis, the site of the famous oracle of Apollo.

Demeter: daughter of Cronos, sister of Zeus, and goddess of agriculture.

Dionysos: another name for Bacchus.

Dirce: a spring near Thebes named after the woman who married Lycus, king of Thebes, after he divorced Antiope. When Antiope became pregnant by Zeus, Dirce suspected an affair between her and Lycus, imprisoned Antiope, and treated her cruelly. Antiope escaped and bore Amphion and Zethus, who besieged Thebes, put Lycus to death, and dragged Dirce over the rocks until the gods in pity for her changed her into that fountain.

Doris: a country of Greece south of Thessaly and home of one of the important Greek tribes. (Dorian is the adjective.)

Dryas: a king of Thrace and the father of Lycurgos, who was driven mad by Bacchus.

Eidothea: wife of Phineus, king of Thrace (sometimes Idothea or Idaea).

Eleusis: a town fourteen miles west of Athens where the Eleusinian mysteries were celebrated in the temple of Demeter.

Erinnyes: spirits of divine vengeance; also called the Eumenides.

Eteocles: son of Oedipus and Jocasta, and brother of Polyneices, Antigone, and Ismene.

Eteoclus: one of the seven against Thebes.

Euboea: a large island off the Greek mainland opposite Boeotia and Attica.

Eumenides: the "gracious ones"; also called the Erinnyes or the Furies.

Euridyce: wife of Creon of Thebes.

Fame: sometimes called Fama, worshiped as a deity and represented as blowing a trumpet.

Fates: the three goddesses Clotho, Lachesis, and Atropos, who determine the course of human affairs.

Fortune: sometimes called Fortuna, whose statue in Achaia held the horn of plenty in one hand and had a winged Cupid at its feet. She is sometimes shown with a wheel in her hand, representing her inconstancy.

Furies: see Erinnyes or Eumenides.

Hades: the land of the dead.

Haimon: son of Creon and Euridyce, fiancé of Antigone.

Hecate: goddess of sorcery and witchcraft, she is identified with other divinities, Selena in heaven, Artemis on earth, and Persephone in Hades.

Helicon: a mountain range in Boeotia, sacred to Apollo and the Muses.

Hermes: messenger of the gods and the guide of souls departing to Hades.

Hippomedon: one of the seven against Thebes.

Hubris: the sin of pride, which prompts Até, an impious act, which in turn brings on Nemesis, or punishment.

Iacchus: another name for Dionysos.

Ismene: daughter of Oedipus and Jocasta, sister of Antigone.

Ismenos: a river near Thebes, sacred to Apollo.

Ister: the Danube.

Jocasta: wife of King Laius of Thebes, and mother and later wife of Oedipus.

Labdacus: an early king of Thebes.

Laius: a king of Thebes of the line of Labdacus, father of Oedipus.

Lycia: a country in southern Asia Minor.

Lycurgos: king of Thrace, son of Dryas.

Maenads: the Bacchantes.

Megareus: son of Creon and Euridyce and brother of Haimon.

Menoeceus: father of Creon and Jocasta.

Mercy: the Greek goddess was Eleus, who had an altar in Athens.

Merope: wife of King Polybus of Corinth and foster mother to Oedipus.

Muses: the nine daughters of Zeus and Mnemosyne, patronesses of the arts.

Nereids: nymphs of the sea, the fifty daughters of Nereus, the sea god.

Niobe: daughter of Tantalos and sister of Pelops. She taunted Leto with having only two children (Artemis and Apollo) while she had ten sons and ten daughters. Apollo and Artemis killed all her children, and Zeus turned the weeping mother into a stone on Mount Sypilus that, even in summer, was wet with her tears.

Nysa: a mountain near Thrace where nymphs cared for the infant Bacchus.

Oea: the region in which Mount Aigaleos is to be found, opposite Salamis.

Oedipus: son of Laius and Jocasta, raised in Corinth by Polybus and Merope. He returned to Thebes, killed Laius, and married Jocasta.

Oeneus: king of Calydon, father of Tydeus.

Olympia: city in Elis, site of the Olympic Games.

Pallas: a name for Athena.

Pan: son of Hermes and Dryope, a goat from the waist down.

Parnassus: a mountain overlooking Delphi, sacred to the Muses and Apollo.

Parthenopaeus: one of the seven against Thebes

Peloponnese: the peninsula of southern Greece, named after Pelops, the grandfather of Agamemnon and Menelaus.

Persephone: daughter of Demeter who is the bride of Hades and rules there with him.

Phasis: a river in Colchis, now known as the Rioni, that empties into the Black Sea.

Phineus: king of Salmydessus who was tormented by Harpies.

Phocis: a district of Greece on the Gulf of Corinth.

Phoebus: the sun, and a name for Apollo

Pirithous: a chief of the Lapiths, a friend of Theseus.

Pluto: another name for Hades.

Polybus: king of Corinth and foster father to Oedipus.

Polydorus: son of Hippomedon and one of the seven against Thebes.

Polyneices: a son of Oedipus and Jocasta and brother to Eteocles, Antigone, and Ismene.

Poseidon: brother of Zeus and Hades and god of the sea.

Prometheus: a son of the Titan Iapetos, he stole fire from heaven and brought it to earth.

Pythia: the giver of oracles at Delphi.

Pytho: another name for Delphi or, by extension, the oracle there.

Rhea: the mother of Zeus, Poseidon, Hades, Hera, Demeter, and Hestia.

Salmydessus: a promontory of Thrace on the Black Sea.

Sardis: a city in Lydia on the Pactolus River that was a source of gold.

Semele: mother by Zeus of Dionysos.

Sipylus: the mountain in Lydia where Niobe's rock was located.

Sphynx: a monster with a lion's body and the head and breasts of a woman, she perched on a rock outside Thebes and strangled those who could not answer her riddle.

Spirits of Death: the Keres, monstrous females who haunted battlefields and ripped the souls from dying soldiers.

Talaus: father of Hippomedon.

Tantalus: a king of Phrygia, father of Pelops and Niobe.

Tartaros: the lowest region of Hades, where the wicked were sent.

Thebes: capital of Boeotia, founded by Cadmus.

Theseus: king of Athens, son of Aegeus.

Thorician rock: a rock at Colonus named for Thoricus, an ancient hero.

Thrace: the territory north of the Black Sea.

Tiresias: a blind prophet of Thebes.

Tydeus: one of the seven against Thebes.

Victory: Nike, the daughter of Styx and Pallas Athena.

Zeus: son of Cronos and Rhea, he was lord of heaven and father of the gods.

Notes

Oedipus Tyrannos

1. (p. 90) The lines in curly brackets are missing in the Greek. I have made cautious guesses from the context.

Oedipus at Colonus

1. (p. 147) A one-line speech of Oedipus, a two-line speech of Antigone, and a one-line speech of Oedipus are missing here.
2. (p. 224) The lines in curly brackets are missing. These are my guesses from the context.